STUDIES IN ECONOMIC AND S[...]

This series, specially commissioned [...] Society, provides a guide to the current [...] themes of economic and social history in which advances have recently been made or in which there has been significant debate.

Originally entitled 'Studies in Economic History', in 1974 the series had its scope extended to include topics in social history, and the new series title, 'Studies in Economic and Social History', signalises this development.

The series gives readers access to the best work done, helps them to draw their own conclusions in major fields of study, and by means of the critical bibliography in each book guides them in the selection of further reading. The aim is to provide a springboard to further work rather than a set of pre-packaged conclusions or short-cuts.

ECONOMIC HISTORY SOCIETY

The Economic History Society, which numbers over 3000 members, publishes the *Economic History Review* four times a year (free to members) and holds an annual conference. Enquiries about membership should be addressed to the Assistant Secretary, Economic History Society, Peterhouse, Cambridge. Full-time students may join at special rates.

STUDIES IN ECONOMIC AND SOCIAL HISTORY

Edited for the Economic History Society by L. A. Clarkson

PUBLISHED

OTHER TITLES ARE IN PREPARATION

Econometric History

Prepared for
The Economic History Society by

DONALD N. MCCLOSKEY

Professor of Economics and of History,
University of Iowa

MACMILLAN
EDUCATION

First published 1987

Published by
MACMILLAN EDUCATION LTD
Houndmills, Basingstoke, Hampshire RG21 2XS
and London
Companies and representatives
throughout the world

Printed in Hong Kong

British Library Cataloguing in Publication Data
McCloskey, Donald N.
Econometric history.—(Studies in
economic and social history)
1. Economic history
I. Title   II.   Economic History Society
III.   Series
330.9   HC21
ISBN 0–333–21371–8

Series Standing Order

If you would like to receive future titles in this series as they are published, you can
make use of our standing order facility. To place a standing order please contact your
bookseller or, in case of difficulty, write to us at the address below with your name
and address and the name of the series. Please state with which title you wish to begin
your standing order. (If you live outside the United Kingdom we may not have the
rights for your area, in which case we will forward your order to the publisher
concerned.)

Customer Services Department, Macmillan Distribution Ltd
Houndsmills, Basingtoke, Hampshire, RG21 2XS, England.

Contents

Preface

The introduction of economic thinking into economic history, overdue in 1957, is largely accomplished by now. What follows is an account for the benefit of non-economists of what has been done so far. The bibliography, long for a book in this series though short by comparison with a complete one, will suggest the scale of the accomplishment. The text amounts to a running commentary on the bibliography: a specialised bibliography of what has been done by historical economists on a particular theme might begin with the citations in the text.

The account is written by a participant, which gives it the advantages and disadvantages of contemporary history. I have tried to be fair, but it is impossible at this range to be Olympian. We will not know for another century or two where the cycle of revisionism on American slavery or British entrepreneurial failure will come to rest. In the meantime we can only note the ways in which economists have altered the terms of the debates.

For no very good reason the piece has taken embarrassingly long to write, in odd moments over many years. The three editors who have seen it from conception to creation – L. A. Clarkson, T. C. Smout and the late Michael Flinn — were extraordinarily patient with my delays. Stanley Engerman and Lance Davis provided me with useful comments on the penultimate version. Various seminar audiences have heard versions of it, and set me on the right path. I thank especially the long-suffering members of the Economic History Workshop at the University of Chicago, who have heard versions of it several times.

Editor's Preface

When this series was established in 1968 the first editor, the late Professor M. W. Flinn, laid down three guiding principles. The books should be concerned with important fields of economic history; they should be surveys of the current state of scholarship rather than a vehicle for the specialist views of the authors; and, above all, they were to be introductions to their subject and not 'a set of pre-packaged conclusions'. These aims were admirably fulfilled by Professor Flinn and by his successor, Professor T. C. Smout, who took over the series in 1977. As it passes to its third editor and approaches its third decade, the principles remain the same.

Nevertheless, times change, even though principles do not. The series was launched when the study of economic history was burgeoning and new findings and fresh interpretations were threatening to overwhelm students – and sometimes their teachers. The series has expanded its scope, particularly in the area of social history – although the distinction between 'economic' and 'social' is sometimes hard to recognise and even more difficult to sustain. It has also extended geographically; its roots remain firmly British, but an increasing number of titles is concerned with the economic and social history of the wider world. However, some of the early titles can no longer claim to be introductions to the current state of scholarship; and the discipline as a whole lacks the heady growth of the 1960s and early 1970s. To overcome the first problem a number of new editions, or entirely new works, have been commissioned – some have already appeared. To deal with the second, the aim remains to publish up-to-date introductions to important areas of debate. If the series can demonstrate to students and their teachers the importance of the discipline of economic and social history and excite its further study, it will continue the task so ably begun by its first two editors.

L.A. CLARKSON

Editor

The Queen's University of Belfast

1   What It Is

It is the part of economics, history and economic history that uses economics to understand the past. As such things go the thing is new.

Fifty years ago only a thin, bright stream of people trained in economic methods used them on history: in the 1930s only Eli Heckscher in Sweden did so, with Earl Hamilton in the United States and a few economists in Britain. In the early 1950s the list was not much longer: it would include Alexander Gerschenkron, Douglass North and Walt Whitman Rostow in the United States; Walther Hoffmann in Germany; and A. K. Cairncross, Brinley Thomas and T. S. Ashton in Britain. Economists were interested in the present rather than in the past. An ahistorical frame of mind was to be expected in the decades of great depression and world war. Historians for their part were fully occupied with literary sources. And the cultivators of the hybrid field of economic history had enough to do without troubling themselves with the higher reaches of economic theory.

In the late 1950s, however, a group of young American economists turned their techniques on history, creating an 'econometric history' (among its many names). So: the subject is a movement in economic history since the late 1950s that has brought modern economics to bear on history.

Although the economics involved has often been simple, the use of even simple economics appears to require professional training. It has long been known that:

> The economic theory we [economists] are using is the theory most of us learned as [first-year students at university]. The reason Ph.D.'s are required is that many economists do not believe what they have learned until they have gone to graduate school and acquired a vested interest in marginal analysis. [Enthoven, 1963, *422*]

Econometric historians have been with few exceptions professionally socialised in economics, not history. Some hold joint
appointments in departments of history and departments of
economics (departments of economic history *per se* do not exist in
North America); a few have professional training in history short of
the doctorate. But most are trained exclusively as economists and
employed exclusively in departments of economics at one of North
America's many hundreds of universities. Most departments of
economics in the United States and Canada have at least one econometric historian on their staffs.

Econometric historians, then, think like economists and talk like
economists. Since by far the largest producer of economists in the
quarter century past has been the United States, they are usually
Americans. These sociological details matter. Many of the charac-
teristics of econometric history arise from the professional and
national character of such folk, American economists trained in
mathematical methods since the Second World War.

The various names under which the movement travels testify to
its character. 'Econometric history' is a coinage of the early 1960s,
out of use except in the title of this book. The word 'econometrics'
means the application of mathematical statistics to economics, and
usually has nothing to do with history. Econometrics was itself
novel in the late 1950s. Since then many doubts have arisen of the
ability of econometrics to deliver the goods it promises. But the
young historical economists were full of the new enthusiasm, and
wished to appropriate its prestige for their movement. Their uses of
mathematical statistics were elementary. Robert Fogel's seminal
book published in 1964, *Railroads and American Economic Growth*,
subtitled *Essays in Econometric History*, contained much good history
and economics, but econometrically speaking only two elementary
fittings of straight lines to scatters of points. A collection in the same
year of their earlier papers by Alfred Conrad and John Meyer,
entitled *The Economics of Slavery and Other Studies in Econometric
History*, was only a little more ambitious in its statistics. 'Econometric history' was merely a verbal ploy of revolutionaries, like
calling one's dictatorship a 'people's democratic republic'.

There are other names. The name '*new* economic history' encap-
sulates the revolutionary heritage. At a conference signalling its
spread to Britain in 1970 Barry Supple recalled those lines on the
French Revolution as it appeared to enthusiasts:

> Bliss was it in that dawn to be alive,
> But to be young [and numerate] was very heaven!

The very belligerence with which the revolutionaries advertised their novelties was again peculiarly American (or French or German; but certainly not British).

The name by which it is affectionately known among the cadre, 'cliometrics', exhibits another, more charming peculiarity, a sense of humour. The word itself is a joke, coined by a mathematical economist friendly with some of the early practitioners: to the muse of history he joined the metrics of 'econometrics'. It is a genial if not especially funny witticism by revolutionaries amused at their own claims to the mantle of Science.

None of the names is very good. 'Econometric history' may connote the right blend of history and economics to a historian, but to an economist it means 'applying *complex* statistical tools to history'. The tools, we shall see, are usually simple and usually not even statistical, as is true in fact of most argument in modern economics. 'New economic history' is beginning to look a little tattered as the movement begins its fourth decade. One cannot go on calling an intellectual movement 'new' that is now the establishment in economic history in the United States and Canada, with strong representation elsewhere in the world.

'Cliometrics' is too easily construed from the Greek to mean simply quantitative history, rather than the quantitative *and theoretical* history *of economies*. Quantitative political and social history, to be sure, have much in common with quantitative economic history. All the quantitative histories draw on the corresponding social sciences and expect the quantitative skills of their practitioners to match the social scientists. But quantitative economic history has different origins – in economics itself rather than history – and has different outcomes. Historical accuracy requires one to distinguish the other new histories from the economic kind.

A fresh attempt at coinage is called for. Most work badly. 'Economic economic history' emphasises the truth that all that is involved is the reintroduction of economics into economic history, but looks like a misprint. 'Histronomics' would give much amusement to methodological reactionaries. The best of a bad lot is 'historical economics'. Even it will awaken in some minds irrelevant echoes of the so-called 'historical school' in the economics of the last century. But it comes closest to the stating plainly what is at stake. Let it be, then, 'historical economics'.

A full definition would go as follows. Historical economics always applies economic theory and therefore commonly involves quantitative ideas, even if not always actual counting. It applies the theory to history almost invariably in the service of history, not in the service of economics. It sometimes uses simple statistical ideas such as graphs, and less frequently advanced statistics and other devices of the calculator's art. Historical economics is modern economics in the service of history.

Historical economics looks different from the standpoint of each field it borders. The looks are revealing. From its ancestral home in economics it looks simply like the earliest among several examples of intellectual imperialism inaugurated in the 1960s. There is now an economics of law, of anthropology, of politics, of crime, of marriage, even of leisure: the economics of history was merely the first of these aggressive extensions of economics into new fields. Like a Victorian imperialist imbued with evangelical Christianity, the economist fancies himself possessed of Scientific Method, hard-headedness, vision, and a unique spiritual gift – the maximising model of man – which suits him to an imperium over lesser breeds. So too, he reckons, in history.

Historical economics appears to an economist to be 'soft'. He supposes that historical economics has fewer and less firm facts to use than present economics and that its practitioners are less well equipped in mathematical and statistical matters than present economists. Neither supposition is correct, but it is difficult to change minds on the matter. Emulating physicists, economists divide themselves into theoretical and applied branches. Historical economists fall into the lower-status, applied branch. Fortunately, the aura of humanistic learning attaching to anything so madly impractical as the study of the past goes some way towards making up the shortfall.

From history, by contrast, the work of historical economists looks like one of several examples of social science history inaugurated or greatly expanded in the 1960s. Each social science has its devotees in historical studies. Historical geography is the oldest as a self-conscious field, from the 1930s and before devoting itself to the study of land tenure in old agricultures or the study of housing types in old cities. Other historical X-ologies were added in the great

14

expansion of academic life that followed by seventeen years the post-Second World War baby boom. By the 1980s a good department of history might study eighteenth-century Indian smallpox with the tools of the anthropologist, voting behaviour in the British Parliament of 1842 with the tools of the political scientist, and Japanese peasant unrest with the tools of the sociologist. It was natural to consider studying medieval field systems with the tools of the economist.

True, the heavy technical training required to use economics limited the number of people that could come by way of traditional training in history. One can read the works of Edward Leach or Clifford Geertz without being an anthropologist and come away with at least the conviction of understanding; one cannot say the same of the scholarly works of economists such as Paul Samuelson or Milton Friedman. But when it was sensible to bring economics into history it was done with little fuss.

From economic history itself, however, historical economics looked once upon a time like a barbarian invasion, and caused a very great fuss indeed. Barbarous hordes came roaring out of the west (the usual home of intellectual barbarians), calculators thumping on their thighs and computer paper flowing from their packs. Rudely seizing the harvest of the native historians and sticking it into a porridge disgusting to civilised taste, they sat down to feast amidst grunts of 'we hypothesise that the coefficient will be significantly different from zero at the .05 level'. Frightful stuff.

One of the barbarians put it well in 1968, on the eve of the invasion of Britain: 'And It Will Never Be Literature.' In the early days a distinguished British economic historian asserted to a lecture in London that the historical economists were 'illiterate'; a cheeky member of the audience (significantly, he was young, American, an economist, and decidedly illiterate) replied loudly that the Old Economic Historians in their turn were 'enumerate'.

Such controversies within economic history, and such puerile name-calling, have died down of late. The victims of the invasion have become tolerant of economic standards of logic – and many had been tolerant of methodological diversity anyway. The invaders themselves, as happens, assimilated the tastes if not always the language of the natives. The best of the historical economists have achieved standards of fact worthy of the best historians – and many had been catholic in their methodological faiths anyway.

Above all, the controversies about the feasibility of historical economics have died down in the 1980s because it has worked. A *Bibliography of Historical Economics 1957–1980* [McCloskey and Hersh, 1987] compiled using a narrow definition of the field, contains over 4500 citations of essays and books. A recent count of cliometric articles in journals concerning British history alone in the years 1967 to 1981 found 268 [Lee, 1983]. The number grows exponentially.

In the face of such evidence it seems pointless to go on claiming that historical economics is impossible, or even very peculiar. Historical economics is no longer a mere proposal. It has decisively shaped many historical controversies, among them the functions of European manorialism, the reasons for open fields, the dimensions of the industrial revolution, the significance of the nineteenth-century innovations in transportation, the quality of Victorian entrepreneurs, the character of American slavery, the nature of British rule in India, and the causes of the Great Depression of the 1930s. It does history.

Around 1970, though, one might have thought that the feasibility of historical economics was a wholly philosophical matter (McClelland, 1975, is a sophisticated survey). The true believers talked excitedly of a scientific history, of the meaninglessness of non-quantitative evidence, of the promise of economic theory. The sceptics talked of the ultimate unpredictability of humankind, of the meaninglessness of quantitative evidence, of the glories of historical *verstehen*. The debate was entirely philosophical and theoretical: as we say, 'highbrow'.

The highest of the highbrow debates dealt with 'counterfactuals'. A counterfactual is a thought experiment: 'what would have happened *if*?' The historical economists, especially Robert W. Fogel, argued that any serious inquiry into why the industrial revolution happened or how much difference the invention of the railway made to American economic growth would involve a counterfactual. One cannot tell how much X matters without at least implicitly telling what would happen *without* X. Since X did actually happen – accumulation of machines and buildings did happen during the industrial revolution, the railway did in fact get invented – the inquiry into 'without X' (without the industrial revolution or without the railway) requires a step into a hypothetical, counterfactual world of things that did not actually happen. Historical economists see no alternative to speaking counterfactually if one wishes to speak of the causes. Indeed, they believe they see historians themselves using counterfactuals daily.

Such talk outraged the early critics of historical economics, and impelled them to add to their senior-common-room disquisitions on its impossibility a set of bright remarks about 'preferring to deal in what actually happened rather than in figments'. Philosophers themselves had worried about the counterfactual, or the 'contrary-to-fact conditional', well before Fogel, but had exhausted their energies on word puzzles tangential to the uses of the thing. At the practical level the most trenchant criticism of the use of the counterfactual is that it entails an infinite regress [Elster, 1978, *ch. 6*]. One wishes to know what American income in 1890 would have been without the railway. But the railway itself had causes, and those causes in turn had causes, and so on back to the Creation. A world that did not invent the railway in the early nineteenth century and apply it successfully in the middle nineteenth century would not have been our world, but some other. It is not obvious that it would have had the other actual features of our world. It might possibly have been a world in which the sea was boiling hot and in which pigs had wings; on both counts the system of transport would have been different, and incomparable.

As is apparent from the onward rush of historical economics, though, such highbrow objections are not decisive, or even very interesting. A counterfactual can be reasonable or unreasonable, entailing a thought experiment that is researchable ('What if the steamboat had not been invented until 1850?') or not researchable ('What if the industrial revolution had not happened?'). That counterfactuals in some ultimate sense are self-contradictory or that economic models in some ultimate sense abstract from the whole of human nature or that people in some ultimate sense are free and indescribable by deterministic models – all these are philosophical points mainly irrelevant to writing persuasive history.

It should be noted that the highbrow ruminations of historical economists *contra* 'old' economic history are also irrelevant. That non-quantitative evidence could conceivably be reduced to quantity is beside the point in a world without the time or incentive to perform the reduction. That history may some day have the character that the speaker imagines to be 'scientific' is beside the point of doing history now.

One still occasionally reads ruminations of an amateur philosophical sort about historical economics in the pages of American economics journals or, from the Luddite side, in the pages of the *Times Literary Supplement*. They are usually inferior to what a bright second-year student could devise for a weekly essay, and nowadays are blessedly rare. The *methodenstreit* of the early years of historical economics was fruitless, now ended. To repeat, the useful question, surely, is not philosophical but practical. It is, what has historical economics done?

2 The Uses of Economic Theory

Historical economics does what it has done by means of economic theory. A quarter of a century before the first stirrings of historical economics the great Swedish economist and historian, Eli Heckscher, put it this way:

> Now, if economic theory is at all what it ought to be, its reasonings should apply to economic life as such, and consequently to that of all ages. No doubt much remains to be done in the field of economic theory; but an attempt might at least be made to utilize economic theory for the work of economic history. [Heckscher, 1930]

An historian unable to make use of the intellectual apparatus constructed in the two centuries since Adam Smith may be a fine fellow, an excellent scholar, a skilled user of statistics, an important figure in historical studies, but if innocent of economic theory he will not be doing historical economics.

There is no shame in this, even when the subject is clearly economic: it is possible to do excellent economic history that knows little economics. True, it will often suffer by missing the economist's logic of economic life. But one piece of economic logic is that there is a substitute for most things, and therefore there is a substitute for economic logic in producing good economic history. The historian who is especially imaginative about the use of his sources or especially artful in telling his tale can do fine work without economics. So great is their brilliance in other ways, for instance, that Moses Finley, the leading economic historian of the ancient world, and Fernand Braudel, the leading economic historian of the early modern world, make important contributions without knowing economics.

Ordinary historians will more often require its aid. In the 1960s two groups of economic historians largely unacquainted with economics fell to quarrelling about the effects of a series of good

19

harvests in Britain in 1730–50. They quarrelled over how the good harvests would affect the demand for industrial products like cloth and iron. One group pointed out that the good harvests drove down the price of grain, reducing on balance the income of the farming community. (Notice that even this argument uses the elementary but important piece of economic reasoning that because the demand for grain tends to be 'inelastic' – that is, insensitive to price – a small rise in supply required a large fall in price, to induce buyers to buy, leaving farmers with lower revenues.) Since the farming community was one part of the demand for industrial goods, the demand for industrial goods on that account would be lower. A good harvest therefore was a drag on the industrial revolution. So it was said.

The other group, however, pointed out that on the contrary the fall in price would increase the real income of the non-farming community. (Notice again that the argument uses economic reasoning, that what matters is income relative to the prices of the goods bought – such as farm goods – not money income alone.) The higher real income would result in more purchases of industrial goods (once again by elementary economic reasoning). A good harvest, therefore, was an impetus to the industrial revolution. So it was said.

The debate encouraged the collection of useful information on the links between the agricultural and industrial parts of the eighteenth-century economy. Yet it was inconclusive. In 1975, however, an economist noticed that the two groups of historians were pulling at opposite ends of the same bone [Ippolito]. Educated to contemplate whole economies at once, and to recognise that the income of one part is the expenditure of another, an economist could see that the farmers' loss was precisely the non-farmers' gain. It is no great mental trick. The fall in the farmers' revenue was what non-farmers therefore did not need to pay to acquire grain. The lower income of farmers *was* the higher income of non-farmers. The nation as a whole did not lose or gain income. Therefore industrial goods did not lose or gain. What the demand for industry gained on the swings it lost on the roundabouts. As a first approximation the argument of the first group of historians plus the argument of the second equalled zero.

As a second approximation, to which Ippolito then turned, good harvests increased a little the income of the nation. The nation as a whole is plainly better off when the weather is better. This too illustrates the saturation of the argument with an economic point of view, for the knack of looking through the chaos of claims to the nation as a whole is another result of economic training. Ippolito concluded that the small increase worked to increase demand for industry, but not by much. Both groups of historians were mistaken.

The economic theory applied in historical economics can be, as here, quite simple, not far removed from common sense. Common sense must always keep the upper hand in economic argument as in any other argument, though the correct common sense is seldom the common opinion. Economic common sense is a system of thinking and arguing, not a collection of settled conclusions about the world. Ippolito did not have access to a book of ready-made conclusions about the effect of agriculture on industry. The act of 'applying' economic theory, therefore, is rather different from the engineer applying his knowledge of the strength of materials to a particular bridge or a barrister applying her knowledge of precedent to a particular case. The theory by itself has very little to say about the world. Economists sometimes say 'theory tells us' such and such – for instance, that free trade is desirable. The expression is as foolish as the parallel expression, which sometimes escapes the lips of historians, 'the facts tell us'. Mute facts unarranged by human theories tell nothing; human theories unenlivened by facts tell less than nothing.

That economic theory is a system of argument can be seen in a startling piece of argument by the historical economist E. G. West. The subject was English education in the nineteenth century [West, 1975a, 73–4, 80–3]. By the Forster Act of 1870 England moved from a miscellany of mainly religious schools to a uniform system of state schools, made wholly free in 1891. The Act has been applauded on all sides, and unrefined common sense would agree. Surely it is a Good Thing to provide free education. But West argued that the Act and its sequels may well have been a Bad Thing, supposing that the purpose was to induce the nation to spend more on education.

The argument relies on the elementary economic point: that one day of education is a substitute for any other. As the jargon has it, days are 'fungible'. A day of free schooling is fungible with a day of paid schooling. Therefore an increase in the number of places in state schools will to some degree merely substitute for places in religious or fee-taking schools. Just as the expansion of government charity can be expected to displace some private charity, the expansion of state schools can be expected to displace some non-state schooling.

But West goes further. He points out that a child could not go to a state school and a non-state school simultaneously. Suppose the state school, though free, provided less education – by having, say, larger classes or poorer facilities. Then low- to middle-income parents might well be tempted by the offer of free state education to send their children to the school providing *less* education. The parents would be better off, since it is obviously better to get something free than to have to pay for it. But the children might have received less education by going to state schools. That is to say, it is possible that the total amount of education provided to the children of England actually *declined* relative to what it would have been without the intervention of the state. West found in fact – though he does not claim by this to have proven the case beyond doubt – that the share of income devoted to education per child fell after 1870 in England and Wales, while rising sharply in Germany, France, Italy and the United States.

The reasoning is not controversial in logic. What is controversial is whether or not the logic is applicable to English education in the late nineteenth century. The hard part of arguing economically is selecting the logic likely to be most applicable to the case at hand. To repeat, the economist does not select from a formulary of pre-solved problems, although like everyone else he will argue by means of the analogy of one problem with another.

Notice that the language of economic argument is not necessarily mathematical. No mathematics has been used to describe West's argument. West's article in fact contained no algebra; its tables and graphs would not strike terror into anyone moderately numerate; and its solitary diagram was buried discreetly in a footnote. The method of historical economics is not mere calculation, or higher mathematics. It is arguing – by analogy, example, thought-experiment, dialogue, arguments *a fortiori, a contraris, a definitione*.

Common-sensical though economics can be, learning to argue in this way does not come automatically with experience of life or scrutiny of the *Economist*. Pop economics is not the genuine article. As a way of arguing about society, genuine economics is similar to mathematics (a way of arguing about numbers) or literary criticisms (a way of arguing about novels). No adult would regard herself a master of mathematics because she could count to 100 or of literary criticism because she understood the humour in Pooh, the bear of little brain. But the parallel error is made repeatedly in matters economic, even by adults.

It is commonly supposed that economics is for instance entirely ideological, a mere apology for capitalism, say, or a set of plans for socialism. It is supposed, again, that the gist of economics is a vocabulary, such as 'oligopoly' or 'multiplier', as though sprinkling one's talk with 'non-standard analysis' or 'hermeneutics' would make one an expert in other fields. Economics is not a catechism to be mastered in an afternoon. It is a way of arguing, a difficult though not unreasonable way, and foreign to most politicians and journalists. The public therefore gets no tuition in it from watching public life (for some excellent academic tuition, see Hawke, 1980).

Acquiring the habits of genuine economic argument, of course, is no guarantee of sure-footedness, even in elementary matters. A few instances from the literature on British industry 1870 to 1939 illustrate how economic reasoning can go, and how it can go astray.

The simplest concerns the common sense of costs. British owners of coal-powered ships built before the First World War found themselves after the war losing money in competition with oil-powered ships. The ships earned enough after the war to pay the crews and buy the coal, but not enough to cover all the repayments on the investment in the ships themselves [Henning and Trace, 1975]. Yet the owners carried on. The impulse is to castigate the owners for their irrationality in entering and carrying on a losing proposition.

The impulse should be resisted. The owners were not on this evidence irrational to have entered the business of coal-powered ships. What matters is what they could have rationally expected *when purchasing the ships,* in 1910, say, lacking a crystal ball. The actual outcome is irrelevant. That a bet does not come off does not always indicate that it was a poor bet. Nor were the owners necessarily irrational to carry on even after the dismal future of coal-powered ships was revealed, so long as the ships covered their out-of-pocket costs of operation. The money the owners had to pay their bankers for the construction cost of the ships was fixed and bygone. It had to be paid whether or not the ships moved out of harbour, and was therefore irrelevant to the decision to let them sail. Refined common sense shows that the shipowners might have been sensible to carry on.

The case illustrates, too, the powerful tendency in economics to credit self-interested people such as British shipowners with rationality. The economist supposes that people do things for reasons, not habitually or accidentally or mistakenly. Furthermore, the economist supposes that what people do spontaneously is probably good. The economist is no Dr Pangloss, believing that all is for the best in the best of possible worlds. Yet it must be admitted that he has Panglossian tendencies, to which he will occasionally surrender.

The opposite view, the Legal Fallacy, is that the multitude (when uninstructed by lawyers and politicians) is bound to blunder, and needs therefore the guidance of wise laws framed by wise parliaments and wise courts. All is for the worst in the worst of possible worlds, except in the wise world of government. The government on this view would have been wise to tax steam coal in the 1920s to offset the blundering desire of owners to keep their ships running. The economist's first instinct (though not always his last) is to doubt that present-day lawyers or historians could do much better even in retrospect than the business people of the time.

A somewhat more complex instance of the uses of simple economic reasoning concerns an argument made in 1940, by Duncan Burn. Burn was an influential historian of the British steel industry and an early proponent of the notion that British business enterprise was weak from 1870 onwards. Explaining why British steel companies were slower than German or American companies to introduce large-scale plants, he wrote 'great new plants could emerge in Germany and the States without other plants being stationary, let alone shrinking or disappearing . . . . German and American markets had far larger and more expansive home markets' [1940, *240;*].

The argument is misleading. An individual company is not constrained by the whole market. The size of the market for steel as a whole is irrelevant to Bolckow Vaughan and Company; and Bolckow Vaughan would scarcely care whether Dowlais, the Barrow Haematite Steel Company, or Workington Iron and Steel were shrinking or disappearing. Unless there is only one or a very few companies (there was not) the scale of the market is not a constraint on the growth of any one. In any case British steelmakers in the late nineteenth century were *not* in a narrow market, for they could sell abroad. Their market was the world.

The error might be called the Geographical Fallacy, which is to be piled over in the corner with the Legal one. You buy bread at a particular shop. Were the shop to close you would not go without bread, though you would presumably be inconvenienced by having to shift from your first choice in shops to your second. The geographer might properly view the shift as interesting, it being her concern to study the matching of buyers and sellers. The economist views it as uninteresting. Particular matchings of buyers and sellers, such as Bolckow Vaughan's sales to a particular shipbuilding firm, are in his view relatively unimportant accidents of location and custom. Bolckow Vaughan is not importantly constrained by selling to the particular firm, and will easily find new customers should it wish to sell more (for instance, after building a 'great new plant').

A related example concerns another industry said to have 'failed' in Victorian times, cotton textiles. The great new plants that Britain built in cotton textiles before the First World War proved useless after the war (as indeed they would have in steel). Between 1913 and 1927 British exports of cotton cloth fell from 7100 million to 4200 million yards. India had been the match for nearly half of the British cloth, taking 3200 million yards in 1913. By 1927, after developing its own industry, India took only 1800 million from Britain. Someone in the grip of the Geographical Fallacy would take out her pocket calculator and calculate that the development of India's own industry was responsible for (3200–1800)/(7100–4200) or 1400/2900 or 48 per cent of the decline in British exports.

The calculation, however, is irrelevant. British output fell because the world price of cotton textiles fell, a consequence of many countries including India expanding their industries (notably, Japan and the American South). The particular matching of Manchester cotton firms with Bengali buyers is irrelevant. That Britain in an arithmetical sense 'depended' on India reflects small advantages of political connection, language and habit, not the absolute dependence imagined in the Fallacy (namely: sell to Bengal or sell to no one). Although people believed it at the time, and historians have made the corresponding calculations, Indian development in the 1920s was not responsible for the catastrophes in British cotton textiles.

A more subtle instance of the give and take of economic argument is the alleged burden of Britain's early start. It is said that Britain, being the first to industrialise, was burdened with old machinery and plant, making up-to-date investment difficult. A leading case is that of the tiny coal wagons on the railways. The wagons were large outside of Britain, especially in Germany and America, and large ones were said to be cheaper to use. As early as 1915 the American economist Thorstein Veblen could write of the tiny British wagons as a scandal of irrationality, or at least industrial senility, Britain clinging to its antique habits while younger industrial nations adapted. Later economists elaborating on Veblen's argument have attributed the delay to 'interrelatedness', which is to say that the coal wagons rode on interrelated equipment (the sidings, track, terminals, shunting facilities) which would also need replacement if big wagons replaced small [Frankel, 1955; Kindleberger, 1964, *141–5*]. The natural disinclination to remodel an entire system to suit new wagons was made firmer by an institutional peculiarity of the British system: the collieries owned the wagons and the railway companies owned the rest.

What puzzles an economist about such an analysis is that the institution survived. Shades of Dr Pangloss: what exists might well have a good reason; or at any rate its reason is worth some thought. The institution did not have to survive. The railway companies could have bought up the obsolete wagons; or begun haulage companies of their own, fitted out with big, new ones; or offered some of the gains from the bigger wagons to the collieries as an inducement to switch; or pressured the collieries with new regulations. None of the tales of irrationality offers evidence that such changes of the institutions were tried and found impractical. To this day, forty years after a nationalisation that presumably got around the bad old interrelated institutions the coal wagons remain tiny. New ones are still being built. A Panglossian thought: perhaps the tiny coal wagons were not so expensive to operate after all.

The failure to consider such a line of thought might be called the Sociological Fallacy. One more for the pile in the corner. It supposes that institutions do not adjust to market conditions. Of course sometimes they do not. Like the Legal and Geographical Fallacies, the Sociological Fallacy is fallacious only when it is not a great truth. Sometimes the separation of ownership from control on the railways *can* prevent progress; sometimes the forms of land tenure or the traditions of the workplace or the organisation of business firms *do* prevent the market from achieving a good equilibrium. The fallacy is dangerous only if one assumes that such institutions are always rigid and powerful and that the market is always weak. Or rather it comes from failing to ask where the alleged weakness comes from.

An instance of the Sociological Fallacy is the common argument that rising output of, say, the British cotton textile industry from

1815 to 1860 'spread fixed costs over a larger output and therefore reduced costs per unit'. The argument appears to have an economic cast, and is definite in its mathematics. Even some economists think it pretty. But most find it ugly, a gross perpetration of the Sociological Fallacy. An economist with any sense of craft will feel uncomfortable in its presence, and will search for the source of its ugliness.

She will realise that the argument takes as given and unalterable the institutional fact of the number of cotton textile firms. The industry used 81 million pounds of raw cotton in 1815 and fully 1084 million in 1860. If the institutions *do not adjust their numbers to market conditions,* then the fixed costs of buildings, scutchers, carders, speed frames, spindles, looms and bosses' salaries would have been divided by the ratio 1084/81, or 13.4, as the industry grew. But growing output causes in the normal course of events a growing number of firms. The number of institutions is not given.

Furthermore, each firm reacts to market conditions by producing at its most profitable output (another instance of the assumption of rationality). The cost-spreading argument assumes that the costs of the firm would be lower if it sold more. The most profitable output cannot be an output at which a firm still faces unexhausted opportunities for lowering costs by selling more. Otherwise the firm would wish to sell more. And each firm *can* sell more, as steel firms could: the size of the market was not a constraint on an individual firm. The British cotton industry in the nineteenth century was even more split up among firms than was steel. The output per firm was determined by an unceasing search for profit, not by a mechanical dividing up of a given market amongst a given number of firms.

Like any lively set of ideas, then, economic research is a matter of arguments in a conversation. To the naïve notion of spreading fixed costs the economist gives the reply just given, raising the level of the conversation above arithmetical tautologies. To her remark in turn another economist might reply that the cotton textile industry did in fact exhibit 'economies of industry scale', as it is put. These would be cheapenings of production arising from better training of the workforce or more specialised production of machines – arguments consistent with rationality, if not necessarily important in this particular case. The economists would then shift to factual inquiries. The lack of easy conclusion to the conversation is evidence not of some arbitrary quality in economics but of the complexity of the issues, a complexity gradually revealed by the conversation itself.

A good example of the conversation, involving essentially the same point as the cotton textile problem, is Paul David's analysis of 'The Landscape and the Machine' [1971]. The landscape is the British farm in the middle of the nineteenth century; the machine is the horse-pulled mechanical reaper, invented about 1830 in both Britain and America; the question – all good history has a question – is why the reaper was adopted more slowly in Britain than in America. By 1865 50 per cent of American corn was being cut by machine; the same share was not reached in Britain until ten years later. Why? The usual answer – usual at least among non-economic historians – is that British farmers were more conservative than American farmers. Another case of British irrationality, like real ale and silly mid-off.

Paul David's reply is that on the contrary the British farmers were perfectly rational. Harvest labour was cheaper in Britain. The land itself, having been ploughed up into ridge and furrow for drainage, was not as convenient for a clumsy machine as it was on the plains of Kansas (or the plains of Midlothian, where the machine was also adopted early). Above all, British farms were smaller. The fixed cost of the machine was spread over a smaller acreage, making the per acre and per bushel cost higher.

Other economists might retort that in making the point about small farms David has overlooked the possibility of institutions adjusting to market conditions. He has committed the Sociological Fallacy. David had argued that if a reaper could harvest 100 acres a season a 25-acre farm would find a reaper expensive. The response is that four such farms would constitute profitable business for a reaping company. A company that could reap 100 acres on four farms might not be at much of a disadvantage compared with one farmer on 100 acres reaping by himself.

David might reply again that such companies did not exist in Britain, suggesting that they were in fact at a disadvantage, even if in theory they might not have been. The reply in turn to his reply might be that reaping companies are not the only possible institutional adjustment to the market. Neighbours might club together to buy a machine; Farmer Brown reaping 70 acres might notice that his machine was idle the last week of the harvest, and rent it out to Farmer Smith; or each might increase his grain acreage to take advantage of the new technology. David might reply again that he doubted it, and call for evidence. The others might return again that they, too, had doubts, doubts that the farmers were so agile in response as David argues elsewhere if they could not imagine such simple arrangements. They too would call for evidence, which would need to show that changing the institutions was expensive. So the conversation might go. (And did. See the discussion of David's essay in McCloskey, 1971, *206–14*.) The conversation is not without point merely because it is as yet without sharp conclusion. The understanding of the history is in the end greater even if the end does not reveal a Truth. The conversation continues [McLean, 1973; Olmstead, 1975; Ankli, 1980].

A related issue is the Irish Land Question of the nineteenth century, the question being whether tenants should have been compensated for improvements to the land such as ditching and fencing. If they were not compensated the landlord could profitably evict them, getting a higher rent from a new tenant for the land improved by the tenant's money and sweat. Realising this, the tenants would be reluctant to invest in improvements. Without long leases and fixed rents, it is said, improvements were ignored and Irish agriculture in the late nineteenth century decayed.

The argument has long been considered decisive. The same Paul David brought it back across the Irish Sea to explain why English farmers did not invest in levelling out the land to make it more suitable for mechanical reaping. In the Irish case, though, Barbara Solow has shown that the tenure arrangements were unimportant [Solow, 1971]. To suppose on the contrary without evidence that they were important is to perpetrate again the Sociological Fallacy. Solow assembles evidence that in Irish circumstances a series of short leases were as good as one long one; the tenant and landlord mostly co-operated; the job got done if it was really worth doing. The institutions, in short, were often flexible, and when inflexible they were often unimportant.

Some will complain about such a use of economic theory that it supposes people to be unreasonably close calculators. Farmers are portrayed as making close calculations of land-levelling costs, cotton textile firms of the best output, railway companies of coal costs. The objection is a reasonable one: we see ourselves failing to make the best decision about which food to buy or whether to change jobs. Since most of us wander in a fog of indecision the bright sunlight in which the rational man strides is hard to credit.

Various replies are possible. The brightness needed for rationality is easily exaggerated. An English farmer did not need detailed engineering specifications for each of the dozens of reaping machines available in order to make up his mind to buy. Nor did he need perfect foresight about the future price of harvest labour. A crude decision is rational if information to make a more subtle one is expensive. If it were profitable to do so the market itself would make available some of the information, by means of catalogues and commercial travellers. The decision-makers in question were not consumers making many trivial decisions about toothpaste and tea; they were producers making a few decisions about what big machine to buy, decisions on which their livelihood depended. Such a producer would have every incentive to think clearly. Further, the clarity need characterise only some of the decision-makers. Most could have been lumpish and driven by habit, letting their livelier cousins show the way.

Above all, the assumption of close calculation can be tested. It is not an assumption removed from scrutiny. The entire point of David's calculation was in fact to scrutinise it. One can make the same calculation for the unimportance of who owned coal wagons or Irish land, the irrelevance of matchings in the cotton or iron market, the fungibility of state and denominational schools, the offsetting effects of harvests. The postulate of close calculation can be tested.

Indeed, if the leading question in historical economics to date had to be put in one sentence it would be: 'How well does the assumption of close calculation fit the economic past?' The answer has been, 'Well; or at any rate better than earlier students of the matter have believed.' The 'postulate' of rationality in economics is not really a postulate in the Euclidean sense, an allegedly indubitable premise from which irrefutable conclusions can be drawn. It works merely as a working proposition, subject to testing and revision to suit the case at hand. From the outside economics looks deductive, an instance of the deductive certitude that Western intellectuals have pursued since Plato. But for practical purposes the deductive chains of reasoning in economics are short, beginning and ending with links of fact. When an economic argument is mistaken or irrelevant it is usually because it got the facts wrong. The objection that economics 'assumes' rationality is naïve. The facts can speak to the assumption, pro or con.

Another objection to historical economics is that economic theory reduces humankind to a diagram or a mathematical equation. You will note, however, that no diagram or mathematical equation has yet appeared. The reason, to repeat, is that most of the arguments of economic thinking do not need them. Mathematics gives a nice notation, and the journals of economics are crammed with it. But most of the ideas in economics can be expressed as little stories of entrepreneurs buying up coal cars or negotiating shares of a reaper. Most were invented that way.

Still, there is no point in ignoring the formal side of economics. The formalities are important to many of the achievements of historical economics, and none is beyond the power of words. All of the examples given so far can be put mathematically.

The effect of the offer of free state schools on the choices faced by parents, for instance, can be put in terms of the geometry of 'budget lines'. Look carefully at Figure 1, which shows the combinations of education and of other goods that the Supple family could consume in 1869. In the absence of free schooling the Supples had to stay in the

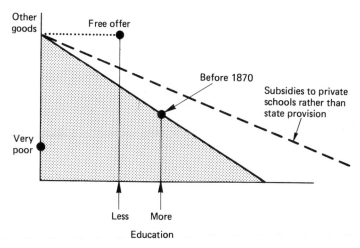

The point 'Free offer' may be reckoned by the Supples to be superior to the point 'Before 1870', even though it entails a fall in the amount of education.

Figure 1. Scarcity of income is represented by a budget line inside which the Supple family must stay

shaded area below the Supples' budget line: they could have more education only at the cost of giving up quite a lot of other goods. Think about that for a moment. This is what it means to 'make a sacrifice' to send children to school. A Teeside song before free schools laments:

> My daddy was a miner and lived down in the town,
> 'Twas hard work and poverty that always kept him down.
> He aimed for me to school but brass he couldn't pay
> So I had to go to the washing rake for fourpence a day.
>
> [MacColl, 1954]

From the Supples' point of view the offer of free schooling adds the point labelled 'Free offer' to the opportunities. The Supples can now have their cake and eat it too, taking the free offer of schooling and devoting all their income to other goods. So the Supples are made better off. Pause to savour this point. But while taking up the state's free offer the Supples cannot also buy education in the market place: they can either take the state's offer and move to 'Free offer' or refuse it and send their children to fee-taking schools. The children cannot go to both schools at once. They can *either* accept the free offer *or* stay on the old budget line: they cannot do both.

Now the pay off in reasoning. Suppose that before 1870 the Supples were consuming at 'More education' in the figure. The paradoxical-sounding result that E. G. West drew attention to is that after 1870 they may have consumed less. The point 'Free offer' may make them in their own opinion better off on balance (if less educated) than the point 'Before 1870'. But they, and the nation, end up consuming 'Less education'. End of proof.

Figure 1 makes clear at least that the logic is correct, adding conviction to the verbal argument. It is a figure of speech. Like any good figure of speech the diagram suggests extensions of the argument. For instance, the boy at the washing rake was not at the point labelled 'Before 1879': he was at 'Very poor', because his budget line was low. He consumed no education at all. Such very poor people were induced by free education to take more education, not less. One of West's arguments, however, is that fewer people than is usually believed were in such a position, and even those who were in it could have been better helped by direct subsidies. Most English families, he claims, purchased some education before 1870.

32

Figure 1 makes clear another of West's points. Unlike the new system of state schools the older system of state subsidies to private education had unambiguously induced more education to be purchased. The dashed budget line represents a more favourable trade off of education for other goods, more favourable because subsidised by the state or the Church of England or a local charity. Since the budget line is further out and education is made cheaper, more would be consumed. The offer by the state of free education replaced a system that had made buying additional education especially attractive.

The diagram even suggests a technical flaw in itself. The free offer is not really free. Someone must give over the resources to build the schools and feed the teachers. The Supples might receive such a subsidy from outside, but if they are to stand for the nation there is no one outside to give. Pogo was a wise possum in an American cartoon strip long ago. At the end of an episode reminiscent of the Woozle hunt in *Winnie the Pooh* he remarked: 'We has met the enemy and he is us.' So is we. We are it. The nation cannot get outside the budget line to offer itself Free offer. The nation must tax itself. The nation as a whole, then, does not exactly move to 'Free offer', but to some point on the original budget line with Less education than More. The correction of the argument introduces the question of how the 'free' schools were financed. Local rates, it might be argued, fell on property owners, meaning that people with children but without property were net beneficiaries of the state system. In any event the issue is more complex than it seems at first sight, a frequent result of economic conversation. To get further one must turn to empirical estimates of the actual dimensions of the diagram [West, 1975b].

The geometric and algebraic panoply of economics is forbidding, then, but entails no wisdom inaccessible to mortals. Like verbal economics, the formalities of economics are often suggestive of historical arguments that might have been overlooked.

The idea of a budget line just used, for example, is a powerful aid to the imagination. Consider the puzzling frequency before the industrial revolution of holidays and short working hours. One might suppose that the people of Europe in 1700, being very poor, would have had to work very hard to get their bread. But they did not in fact work very hard. Neither did they get much bread: they were poor in goods but rich in free time. The solid line in Figure 2 represents the budget line between consumption goods and hours free from work: by giving up hours one gets bread, housing, clothing. The solid budget line represents the constraint imposed by technique and resources on the amount of goods (the vertical axis) producible from hours (the other axis). As in the case of the Supples, the society is constrained to stay within the budget line. Were it the only constraint, pre-industrial Europe would have chosen the point 'Good day's work'.

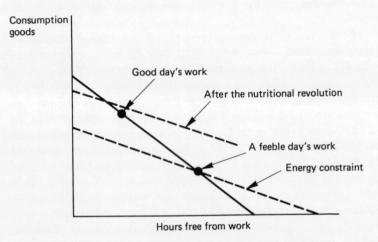

The energy constraint may have prevented Europeans from working hard and long

Figure 2. The constraints on pre-industrial Europe can be thought of as budget lines

But there was another constraint, that on the sheer energy to live and work. As is the case in very poor countries nowadays, argue Herman Freudenberger and J. G. Cummins [1976], bad nutrition meant that Europeans in 1700 were also constrained by the dashed 'Energy constraint' (ignore momentarily the dashed line marked 'After the nutritional revolution'). Both constraints operated. Geometrically speaking, a worker had to stay within *both* budget lines, not merely within the solid one. The best the worker could do, then, was 'A feeble day's work.'

With the early improvement in agriculture, and the introduction of such nutritious crops as potatoes, the energy constraint moved out to the dashed line marked 'After the nutritional revolution'. The energy constraint was no longer binding. A worker could now move to the point 'Good day's work'. And that point entails more work (as well as more goods purchased with the work).

The apparent paradox of richer people working more might in this way be resolved. They worked more because being a little richer they now had the energy to work. Freudenberger and Cummins are modest about the force of their argument, which in this form is a mere preliminary to serious study of the facts. But such a study will have in mind the formal apparatus of the budget line and the idea of scarcity which it embodies.

Although often expressed in such diagrams and mathematics, and most easy to manipulate if the languages of figure and formula have been acquired, most uses of theory in economics, as has been stressed, are intelligible without them. The 'theory of rent' is a good example, an uncomplicated piece of reasoning with wide historical uses. The reasoning is that the renters of something to be used commercially will pay what they can earn from it. The commercial thing can be a slave or a patent or an acre of land – land being the classic instance, and the reason it is called the theory of rent. A farmer renting land will be willing to pay more rent to the landlord if the land improves in profitability. The result is that the owners of the land, not mere farmers renting from landowners, get the benefit from an improvement.

The theory of rent allows the measurement of the previously unmeasurable. The benefit from canals built in the American state of Ohio in the early nineteenth century, for example, looks at first virtually impossible to measure. The benefit to the canal companies in profit is not difficult to know, but the benefit to the good people of Ohio in lower costs of transport is very difficult to know. One would need to know how much the costs fell and how much was carried: that is, one would need detailed statistics on how much was carried on the canals, statistics which do not exist. Rough estimates are possible; for later transport improvements, with better statistics, the estimates have in fact been made. But in 'Social Returns from Public Transport Investment: A Case Study of the Ohio Canal' [1970] Roger Ransom used the theory of rent to measure the benefit indirectly. He reasoned that lower costs of transport would have raised the rent that farmers were willing to pay for land close to a new canal. The price of land would therefore have risen. By examining the prices of land before and after the canals Ransom could estimate the elusive social returns.

Similar notions have been applied to the benefit from English enclosures in the eighteenth century [McCloskey, 1975], to American slavery [Yasuba, 1961], to African slavery [Bean and Thomas, 1974; Gemery and Hogendorn, 1974], and to many other matters. The owners of limited resources such as land or slaves or urban building sites are the sole beneficiaries of improvements that increase their desirability. The desirability, therefore, can be measured from their benefit.

The complexities of economic theory are best illustrated by its exemplar, supply and demand. An economist, it is said, is a parrot taught to answer any question with 'Supply and demand'. The mere phrase in truth does a lot of work.

For instance, it affirms that the quantity sold and the price of, say, cotton textiles in New England from 1815 to 1860 were determined not by bargaining or conspiracy or class power but by competition in an anonymous market, that is, by supply and demand. For better or worse, no one intended the price; no one was to blame. So the theory says. According to the economist's way of talking it was no central plan that caused the quantity to rise by a factor of 363 and the price to fall to a quarter of its 1815 level. It was the sum of individual predictions, ambitions and failures. Even at its most vague the theory of supply and demand leads the historian away from the thrilling but misleading notions of pop economics.

The more definite version of the theory will talk of supply and demand 'curves' moving up and down and out. Again geometry. Since the price of cotton textiles from 1815 to 1860 fell relative to other goods, and the demand for cotton textiles certainly moved out, the supply curve must have fallen. A 'falling' supply curve means simply that a given quantity of cotton textiles was offered at a lower price, the sort of lower price that comes from better ways of making the textiles. The theory draws attention to the possible reasons that a supply curve can fall, such as the cheapening of raw cotton and the mechanisation of weaving. And since the quantity grew so much it seems unlikely that the demand curve remained unchanged. Doubtless it moved out (which is to say that at a given price the amount of cotton textiles that people wanted to buy went up). The theory draws attention to possible reasons, such as rises in the incomes of Americans, the cheapening of transport costs (by

36

those same Ohio canals, for instance), and the substitution of American for British cloth. The commonest use of supply and demand is this: to give the historian an orderly list of factors fixing quantities and prices. The list will vary with the product and the date, but again the mere idea of the list will discipline the history.

A still more definite and complex version of the theory will give quantitative weights to the supply and demand curves, as did Robert Brooke Zevin in his essay on 'The Growth of Cotton Textile Production After 1815' [1971]. The theory needs first to be put in algebraic form, in order to accept numbers from the historical record that express how much the rise of income affected demand or how much the fall in raw cotton prices affected supply. Zevin did so, concluding from the calculations that expansions of demand more than supply caused output to grow, especially in the first decade; that four-fifths of the fall in price was caused by technological progress, especially again in the early years; and that the initial disturbances to the industry smoothed out by the 1830s. Supply and demand at its most concrete provides a narrative framework for the history of an industry. Historical economists, as natural experts in supply and demand, have entered upon such histories with enthusiasm [see Fogel and Engerman, 1969].

The height of the complexity in supply and demand is its generalisation to an entire economy [James, 1984]. If you think of the history of a single industry as the outcome of competition in an anonymous market it is natural to think of an entire economy as a collection of such industries. The study of one market is called 'partial equilibrium'; the study of all markets together, 'general equilibrium'.

The pioneer in using the idea of general equilibrium to write history has been Jeffrey G. Williamson, as expert in the study of present-day poor countries as of the economic history of the nineteenth-century. In 1974 Williamson published *Late Nineteenth Century American Development: A General Equilibrium History*, which displayed the economy of the United States in 72 equations. This sounds like a lot of equations, but in fact, as Williamson himself noted, they do not capture much detail. Since Williamson's main interest was in the contrasts between eastern and western regions he distinguished only East and West for most variables, requiring him to leave out the American South. And to keep the argument calculable and lucid he had to confine attention to the markets in labour, capital, part of land, all manufactured goods taken together, and all agricultural goods taken together (leaving out services). Two goods and three 'factors of production' (as economists call the inputs into the making of goods) are made to stand for all the riches of America in cowboys, coal mines, cotton mills, slum housing, iron deposits, ocean fisheries, books, beer, wheat, cheese, office space, primary education, train journeys, and the means to wage war.

But one cannot think about an economy without simplifying. One cannot deal with everything at once. Even a study of the 'partial' equilibrium of supply and demand in an isolated market throws the rest of the economy into a single category of 'all other goods'. The question is not whether to simplify; you must. The question is whether the particular simplification is useful, that is, whether it illuminates or obscures important historical questions.

The discussion of Williamson's findings – such as the finding that the benefit the economy derived from the railways was larger (20 times larger) than reckoned by other scholars – has turned on such judgments. Again the conversation continues, at a more sophisticated level, raised up to this more sophisticated level by the formal methods. One must judge, for instance, whether it is reasonable for Williamson's model to treat railways as not requiring capital. 'Capital' is the stock of buildings, bridges, machines and so forth used to earn income. The larger output from railways in the model causes the rate of accumulation of capital elsewhere in the economy to rise, which is why Williamson observes such a large impetus to income from the railways. But in fact railways were capital-intensive undertakings, absorbing in 1890 some 10 per cent of the nation's stock of capital. In a model that was able to reflect these facts the railways themselves might gobble up the additional accumulation of capital. The conversation turns to a discussion of how important it is to revise the theory.

Historical economics, then, uses economic theory. The economic 'theory' described here is of the sort most economists have in mind when they use the word. It is not the grander sort of thinking about society that qualifies as theory in other circles. Historical economists have on occasion woven grand theory: Mancur Olson in *The Rise and Decline of Nations: Economic Growth, Stagflation, and Social Rigidities* [1982] examined the sources of modern economic stagnation; J. R. T. Hughes in *The Governmental Habit* [1977] examined the sources of modern government; W. W. Rostow in *The Stages of*

Economic Growth [1960] examined the sources of modern economic growth. But most of the work of historical economists speaks at a lower level of generality.

And most of the theory speaks a 'neoclassical' dialect of economics, the prestige dialect in the English-speaking world during the twentieth century. Some pieces of historical economics use other brands of theory, chiefly of German-speaking origin. Stephen Marglin's 'What Do Bosses Do?' [1976] and William Lazonick's 'Factor Costs and The Diffusion of Ring Spinning in Britain Prior to the World War I' [1981] speak in a Marxist way, though with many borrowings from neoclassical economics. Murray Rothbard's *America's Great Depression* [1975] or Lawrence White's *Free Banking in Britain* (1984) speak an 'Austrian' dialect, that is, an anti-statist way. But the differences among economic dialects can easily be exaggerated. When they speak of the same history they often use much the same tools. All these dialects descend from the language of Adam Smith, whether Marxist, Mengerite, or Marshallian.

The Marshallian, British, neoclassical way of talking, a BBC English with special academic privileges, is commonly assailed by other speakers. It is said to be pointlessly mathematical, which it often is; or too narrow in its concerns, which it once was. Above all by being 'static' it is said to be limited. But this it is not. The most naïve version of the accusation of being static, and the commonest, is that neoclassical economics assumes 'given' resources and technology, and therefore will be a poor way of looking at a world in flux and a wretched way of writing history. The accusation depends on a double meaning of 'given': given meaning 'fixed and immovable', the way the mountains are given; or 'given' meaning 'believed by the economic actor to be outside his control', the way the weather is given (though not fixed and immovable). The first, immovable given is what the critics have in mind; the second, psychological given is how the theory in fact uses the word.

A more sophisticated version of the same accusation is that neoclassical economics does not explain the government or the other institutions of the society in its models, and therefore cannot be used to make sense of a history in which institutions change. The accusation was perhaps a fair criticism twenty years ago. But nowadays, partly under the goad of criticism from the institutionally sophisticated students of Marx, Menger, sociology and historical economics itself, the accusation is outdated [Davis and North, 1971; North,

1984; Scheiber, 1969; Temin, 1976b; Lidecap, 1984].

The uses of economic theory in historical economics, then, are methodologically broad. The theory is the refined common sense descended from Adam Smith, spoken in many dialects. The economists' way of talking has been broadened by using it to talk about large and inconvenient objects in the past. Historical economics is theoretical, but its theory is merely a way of conversing, a rich and useful way.

3   The Uses of Statistics

Economic history is of course a counting subject. Sir John Clapham, a British contemporary of Heckscher trained by Alfred Marshall in the economics of the day, remarked in his inaugural lecture for the first Cambridge chair of economic history, that 'it is the obvious business of an economic historian to be a measurer above other historians' [1929, *68*]. Replete with prices and profits, acres and hands, economic life is the most measurable of human activities. Elsewhere Clapham wrote:

> Every economic historian should . . . have acquired what might be called the statistical sense, the habit of asking in relation to any institution, policy, group or movement the questions: how large? how long? how often? how representative? [1930, *416*]

The advice is good for any historian, economic or not. The attempt to produce a number is usually illuminating, even when no number is in the end producible. Counting is a master metaphor. A historian listing the factors causing the American revolution or the English enclosure movement will give more weight to one factor than to another. The very idea of 'more weight' is quantitative, and to settle on one factor or a few as 'more important' than others is to think quantitatively. Quantities are unavoidable. The sixth of the Principles of Clear Statement enunciated by Robert Graves and Alan Hodge in *The Reader Over Your Shoulder* is that 'there should never be any doubt left as to *how much,* or *how long*' [1943, *139*]. Indeed. They exhibit a 'simple, generally accepted' scale of verbal equivalences for nineteen proportions between 100 per cent and zero: if one says that the higher pay for industrial work in 1830 was 'wholly' swallowed up by bad conditions of life and work, one means 100 per cent of it was; if 'practically all', 99 per cent; if 'the greater part', 70 per cent; if 'a small part', 15 per cent – for the last, see Williamson [1981].

Like the use of economic theory, the use of quantification in economic history evokes fear and loathing among those innocent of

41

numbers (to repair such innocence one should repair to Floud, [1979]). The best response, again, will be to give examples that the quantification works – to show, not that it makes other sorts of historical knowing unnecessary, but that it contributes to what is known.

Some of the reactions, though, can be dismissed at the outset. It is often claimed, as we have seen, that quantification dehumanises history. But dehumanisation depends on the humanity of the historian, not on the instruments he uses. The English medievalist, G. G. Coulton, himself not much of a counter, not to say a quantifier, affirmed nonetheless that:

> to weigh carefully every pertinent fact is not an occupation which need blind us to imponderable values; on the contrary, we are not likely to get the imponderables even approximately right unless we are scrupulously just to the ponderables. [1931, *388*]

It is often said, too, that people in olden times were not statistically minded, and that therefore the statistics of their lives have not survived. When the statistics have survived they are said to be full of error and, to use the metaphor that inevitably accompanies such highbrow doubts, 'they cannot bear the weight of calculation erected on them'. The best response is of course that all this remains to be seen. A slight acquaintance with olden people, however, suggests that Augustan tax gatherers and medieval lords were no less preoccupied than is the Inland Revenue with counting what could be extracted from the victims; though in former times they were less ruthless and efficient. Further, the quantitatively minded can argue that thoughtful calculation is precisely what inexact numbers need [Ohlin, 1974]. Ponder the ponderable.

The goodness of statistics in history is best shown by example:

BOSWELL: Sir Alexander Dick tells me that he remembers having a thousand people in a year to dine at his house. . . .
JOHNSON: That, Sir, is about three a day.
BOSWELL: How your statement lessens the idea.
JOHNSON: That, Sir, is the good of counting. It brings everything to a certainty, which before floated in the mind indefinitely.

An early piece of historical economics, part of the thin, bright stream of cliometrics before its invention (built on the work of a still earlier pioneer in the field, William Beveridge), was the counting by E. H. Phelps-Brown and Sheila Hopkins of English wages and prices for seven centuries [1955, 1956]. The undulations of the purchasing power of the wage – rising after the Black Death of 1348, falling during the resurgence of population in the sixteenth century, and rising to earlier heights and beyond in the nineteenth century – are essential materials for any history of the common welfare.

On a smaller scale of time, with more influence on economics and less on history, Milton Friedman and Anna Jacobson Schwartz [1963, 1982] estimated the stock of money in America and Britain over the century past. The work shows brilliantly the use of history to make a point in economics; it was matched a single other time in the history of economics, by Earl J. Hamilton, he of the thin, bright stream. Hamilton's collections of price and money in Spain during the sixteenth and seventeenth centuries [1934, 1936, 1947] made the same economic point as did Friedman and Schwartz, namely, that the money supply drives the general level of prices. Whether the point is true or false these Keplerian collections of statistics have powerfully stimulated historical thinking about the economy.

The simplest form of counting in historical economics is less like Kepler's and more like Tycho Brahe's, raw observation free of theories of social change. Most of the tables in the national abstracts of historical statistics have this atheoretical character: the price of pig iron and the chaldrons of coal exported are raw facts, though not necessarily useful in raw form. The most important collection is the United States Bureau of the Census, *Historical Statistics of the United States,* produced collaboratively by a flock of historical economists and governmental statisticians first in 1949, then in 1960, revised in 1965 and revised again in 1975 with a big two-volume edition celebrating the bicentennial of the revolution against Britain. Having indexes of prices, income, employment, exports, and such like near to hand was important during the development of historical economics in the 1960s and 1970s for all manner of quantitative thinking about the American economy.

The British economy was provided with a comparable collection in 1962 by B. R. Mitchell (with the collaboration of Phyllis Deane), continuing a three-century-old tradition of political arithmetic. Though revised slightly since its first publication, and like *Historical Statistics* a great spur to quantitative thinking, this *Abstract of British*

Historical Statistics needs revision by many hands. No project does more to focus the economic history of a country than the compilation of its statistics, even atheoretical statistics.

But in fact little of what historical economists do by way of collecting statistics escapes the touch of economic theory. One might imagine that mere counting of the labour force would not have much to do with theory. But Stanley Lebergott's *Manpower in Economic Growth: The American Record Since 1800* [1964] is filled with it. One might think, too, that economic theory would not have much to do with numbers of births and deaths. Yet the rapidly growing family of historical economists enthralled by demography, beginning with Richard Easterlin's *Population, Labor Force, and Long Swings in Economic Growth: The American Experience* [1968], have linked land availability and food prices with fertility and mortality in a new and strangely cheerful Malthusianism [Lindert, 1978; McInnis, 1977; Sanderson, 1980; Steckel, 1980; Lee (ed.), 1977; Mosk, 1978; Haines, 1979; Mokyr, 1983; Weir, 1984; Yamamura and Hanley, 1978].

What looks like a simple job of counting must rely on economic theory if it counts any aggregate such as the labour force or, more so, an aggregate such as 'the output of industry'. Measuring an aggregate of shoes and iron and cotton cloth and chemicals must weight in some way the disparate items. Consider for instance the output of three important British industries in 1860 and 1913 given in Table 1.

Table 1: The Aggregation
of the Output of Three British
Industries 1860–1913 is Ambiguous

	Steamships built (thousands of shipping tons)	Pig iron manufactured (millions of tons)	Raw cotton consumed (millions of pounds)
1860	53.8	3.07	1.08
1913	950.	10.3	2.18
Annual rate of growth	5.4%	2.3%	1.3%

Source: Mitchell and Deane [1962, *131, 179, 221*].

It would obviously be senseless to add up the shipping and iron tons and the cotton pounds to get 'the' output of British industry: the result would be $53.8 + 3.07 + 1.08 = 57$ units of nothing in particular. Nor would it make sense to average the rates of growth, giving $(5.4 + 2.3 + 1.3)/3 = 3.0$ per cent per year from industries with different weights in the world: cotton is a bigger industry than iron, and warrants a bigger weight.

Economic theory and common sense suggest that the money values of the outputs should be used as weights: the values are the prices (which measure the desirability per unit, as revealed in markets) multiplied by the quantities purchased in some base year (which measure the number of units on which the desirability was earned). But which values? Theory again speaks. A choice of values must be made, but the choice will affect the rate of growth of 'the' output of industry. If the values in 1860 are used as weights, for instance, cotton will bulk large; if the values in 1913 are used (after 53 years of slower growth in cotton textiles than in other industries) the weight of cotton will be smaller. There is no entirely correct way of adding up the industries, merely ways from this or that point of view. The result is intrinsically ambiguous, a theoretical ambiguity known in economics as the 'index number problem'. An apparently straightforward measurement turns out to involve theoretical economic thinking.

Early monuments to such thinking are the index numbers of British industrial output 1700–1950 compiled by Walther Hoffmann [1940, Eng. trans. 1955] and of Italian industrial output 1881–1913 compiled by one of the master teachers of historical economics, Alexander Gerschenkron [1955, 1962]. They sought to add up the industries, and were well aware of the ambiguities of indexes. Ironically, the works of these participants in the thin, bright stream were later found to suffer from the very problem they diagnosed in earlier attempts. C. Knick Harley showed in 1982 that Hoffmann's index overweighted faster growing British industries 1770 to 1815, chiefly by giving too large a weight to cotton (which was then explosive in its growth). Harley's revision gives a 40 per cent lower growth rate of industry during the industrial revolution, and therefore a doubling of the conventional estimate of the size of industry at its alleged beginning. Gerschenkron, likewise, had dated the beginning of Italian industrialisation in such a way that it seemed to have been stimulated by large investment banks. Stefano Fenoaltea [1969 and forthcoming] shows that Gerschenkron's index fails to reveal early stirrings of growth that took a decade to affect the overall index very much. On such simple applications of theory to numbers depend our understandings of modern economic growth early and late.

The theoretical content of the simplest counting is apparent in efforts to calculate the terms of trade. The terms of trade are, roughly speaking, the price of exports divided by the price of imports. To put it physically, it is how much imports in bushels of wheat a country gets for a given sacrifice of tons of iron exports. Speaking about it involves index numbers and more knowledge of the logic of trade than most historians would care to acquire. It is no surprise that a historically interested economist, Charles P. Kindleberger, produced a study of *The Terms of Trade: A European Case Study* [1956] over a long period. Albert Imlah's book, *Economic Elements in the Pax Britannica* [1958], is more a historian's work, though informed by the best thinking of economists. It is also, incidentally, an example of how much of Britain's statistical history depended on foreigners until the 1960s, especially on Germans and Americans inbued with the methodical traditions of German positivism (Schlote, Hoffmann, Gayer, Rostow and Schwartz [the last three published in 1953 a book in which the early work is brought to a head]).

National income, too, uses economic theory. The Social Accounting Movement has overlapped with historical economics from the beginning. It is older than historical economics, originating after the First World War in the work of Stamp, Bowley, Clark and others in Britain and Simon Kuznets and his collaborators in the United States. In most countries it is now mature. It measures the income of a nation as though the nation were a family or a business, a daring master metaphor wrapped in various other metaphors of economic theory.

In the United States the measurement of national income has been much influenced by the example of Kuznets, who from 1930 onwards produced one damned, thick, square book after another on income and capital. Kuznets taught many of the cliometricians at the University of Pennsylvania, Johns Hopkins University and Harvard, embodying from an early date the idea of cliometrics (though he resisted the application of the word to himself). The work of Raymond Goldsmith [1965], Moses Abramovitz [1956], Edward Denison [1962], John Kendrick, Solomon Fabricant, Geoffrey Moore and others associated with the American National

Bureau of Economic Research has a Kuznetsian character. The estimation of American national income by Robert Gallman, a student of Kuznets, has played an especially large role in American historical economics [Gallman, 1966; Gallman and Howle, 1971]. The earliest American census usable for Gallman's purpose is 1839; earlier estimates, and estimates in other countries, have required still bolder uses of theory to leap across evidential voids [Parker in Conference on Income and Wealth, 1960; David, 1967; Crafts, 1983; Anderson, 1975]. Estimating so refined a statistic as net fixed capital formation, which has been attempted by historical economists in numerous countries [Cairncross, 1953; Bos, 1979; Butlin, 1964; Hoffmann, 1965; Rosovsky, 1961), plainly involves theory: after all, what is net fixed capital formation but the excrescence of an economist's brain?

However stolid their appearance on the printed page, a daring economic argument underlies such numbers. Much of the conversation of scholarship in historical economics consists of revising them. Phyllis Deane and W. A. Cole built up their magnificent statistics for *British Economic Growth 1688–1959: Trends and Structure* [1962 and later editions] from numerous economic arguments, which Nicholas Crafts has lately rethought [Crafts, 1985]. The growth of British income in the eighteenth century is gradually coming into focus, and appears to be slower than was once thought (fitting Harley's views on industry just mentioned). The British statistics of income and capital since the eighteenth century have been the work of Charles Feinstein, largely singlehanded [1972, 1978]. Again they have shown slower growth, analysed in detail in a more recent sequel to Deane and Cole, *British Economic Growth 1856–1973* [1982] by R. C. O. Matthews, C. H. Feinstein and J. C. Odling-Smee.

The collection of historical statistics has been motivated more often by curiosity about generalisations – Growth in Modern Times – than by curiosity about the past for its own sake. Though with a good claim to being another of the thin, bright stream of early historical economists [1954], Feinstein's collaborator, R. C. O. Matthews, is best known in economics for his work on the theory of economic growth, a theory that even from his pen has been notably free of worries about its historical veracity [Solow and Temin, 1978]. Phyllis Deane, likewise, began her study of history long past with an interest in the recent economic growth of poor countries, a popular subject in the post-imperial 1950s. Kuznets was the leading student of modern economic growth for fifty years, but journeyed into the past to frame general truths for the future. It seems strange at first that the number-makers in the field are more concerned than are the theory-spinners with generalising about Economic Behaviour. They make their numbers in aid of a Science of Behaviour.

Non-historical economists, whether or not they accept the implicit analogy with physics, have no substantial interest in history. A few historical experiments are set problems for economics, but it surprises outsiders how few they are. Economics is surprisingly ignorant of the history of the economies it studies. Sometimes an economist will know a little about the aggregate history of economic growth, though 'growth theory' has been satisfied with 'stylised' and erroneous facts. Again, the supposed lag of wages behind prices in earlier times of rapid inflation has engaged the attention of economists [Kessel and Alchian, 1959; Mokyr and Savin, 1976]. 'Hyperinflation', likewise, can only be studied with Central Europe in the 1920s in mind [Webb, 1984]; and the Great Depression of the 1930s still haunts the modern student of booms and busts [Temin, 1976b; Schwartz, 1981; Brunner (ed.), 1981; Wicker, 1982; Mercer and Morgan, 1972; Moggridge, 1962]. For the most part, however, economists are economical in their use of observations, in a way that would seem strange to an astronomer or a geologist. A handful of figures from the latest *Economic Report of the President* is all the factual nourishment they appear to need.

Historical economists, by contrast, exhibit their peculiarity amongst economists by being hungry for facts, even facts with no relevance to last week's headline. A mild interest in early policy towards the natives of the United States might well arise from recent Indian militancy, but a detailed study of the Dawes Act and its perverse effect on Indian farming, important as it is for understanding American history, is not something an economist transfixed by today's newspaper would bother to do [Carlson, 1978]. It is not the economist's usual reaction to an intellectual problem to call for more facts. The massive projects of observing facts that historical economists have recently embarked on, often in aid of estimates of national income and wealth, reflect the self-education of historical economists as historians. They use new sources with the relish a historian would: such as records of the Mormon Church [Kearl, Pope and Wimmer, 1980] or of wealth at death in colonial America

[Jones, 1980] or of occupations in eighteenth-century England [Lindert, 1980].

And yet it is hard to forget that these people are economists, even when they are doing simple counting not informed obviously by economic theory. Their talk is always informed at least by the theory of counting, statistics. Economists are at ease with statistics, and are trained to think statistically.

The historical economist, for instance, finds it easy to resist the historian's urge to collect every single scrap of evidence. From a boy he is trained to sample. The youthful habit has the merit of efficiency. After getting some absolutely large and random sample of observations of the prices of prime-age American male slaves in 1860 – as small as 100, say – little is to be gained in additional accuracy by getting still more. The 101st observation gives much less additional precision than the 10th, even though the 100 are a trivial proportion of the 4 million American slaves. Statistical theory shows that, oddly, the proportion does not matter to the accuracy of a sample. That public opinion polls are taken on a tiny proportion of the public is irrelevant to their accuracy. All that matters is the absolute number of interviewees. Conventionally, a sample as low as 30 is said to be 'large' for purposes of estimating an average.

To be precise, the accuracy of a sample, so long as it is taken at random – entirely without system or bias – varies inversely with the square root of the absolute number in the sample. If the price of slaves in various places actually deviated from its national average of $1500 by $100 about two-thirds of the time, then the so-called 'standard deviation of the population' would be about $100. Suppose you are interested in the 'true' average of slave prices in the South. The precise statistical theory says that the accuracy one could expect from a sample of 100 prices would be the $100 standard deviation of the population divided by the square root of the sample size.

This is the crucial formula. On it great edifices of statistical theory are built. Notice that it divides the sample average by the square root of the number of items in the sample. Therefore, the bigger the sample the greater the accuracy of the estimated ('sample') average, which of course makes sense: more information is good. The formula says that for a sample size of 100 the true, underlying average would be within $100/10 = $10 about two-thirds of the time. Notice that this $10 is already a pretty small error out of $1500.

A larger sample – of say 900 – gathered presumably at nine times the expense of the sample of 100, would by the same formula give an accuracy of $100 divided by the square root of 900 (which is 33). The estimate of the average would vary so far as $100/33) = $3.33 two-thirds of the time. The error from the big sample of 900 is smaller, one-third of the probable error to be expected from the sample of 100: namely, a $3.33 probable error out of the $1500 average rather than $10 out of the $1500. But considering that the little sample was already accurate enough for most purposes – a $10 error out of $1500, to repeat, is not very big – the lower error for most purposes will hardly be worth the nine times greater expense.

The economist therefore is blessedly free of the anxiety, haunting the historian, that the next case will reverse the conclusions: after 30 or 100 randomly selected cases the economist, or any statistically trained person, stops looking. It seems at first odd that economists have such faith in figures. Odd and repellent: 'the age of chivalry is gone. That of sophisters, economists, and calculators has succeeded; and the glory of Europe is extinguished forever.' But the new faith is a reasoned one, based on this law of the inverse square root.

Another instance of it is the faith in estimates of national income, estimates built up from confessedly error-ridden fragments. The fragments relate to separate parts of the nation's expenditure, as in Charles Feinstein's reconstruction of British expenditure back to 1870: add up government spending, investment, stock building, exports and consumption, itself added up from categories such as food consumption, drink, housing, clothing, and so forth [Feinstein, 1972]. Each fragment may be in error by some large percentage – say by as much as plus or minus 45 per cent of the truth two-thirds of the time. Yet the sum of many fragments, being virtually a sample with many items namely, nine), has by the inverse square root law a considerably smaller error. With nine fragments of expenditure the error in the sum of the nation's expenditure would be the square root of 9 divided into the typical error of the fragments, or 45 divided by 3: a 15 rather than a 45 per cent error. Out of components with quite large errors is produced a sum with reasonably small errors.

The reason the sum is more accurate than its components, of course, is that errors in the components will tend to offset each other, half or so being above the truth and half or so below.[1] This is what makes the inverse square law work. The first census of population of British India, for instance, was a remarkably detailed and solid-looking product of imperial administration. The historian would remind us that when all is said and done the village watchmen who filled out the forms put down any figure that came into their heads. The statistician, though, would remind us that so long as the watchmen were unbiased in their estimates the sum of hundreds of thousands of such wild guesses would nonetheless be very accurate indeed.

The reasoned faith in figures of national income has a theoretical prop, too, the 'theory' being another bit of common sense elaborated. It is the Micawber Rule: that what one expends must be equal to what one earns, and likewise for the nation. Since they are merely two sides of the same sheet in an accounting of income and expenditure the nation's expenditure in millions must add up to the nation's income in millions. Life being what it is, of course, the one never quite adds up exactly to the other; the odd million will be misplaced. From 1948 to the present in the British national accounts the discrepancy has been only 1 per cent or so, adding conviction to both figures; but in Feinstein's painstaking estimates 1870–87 the discrepancy is fully 14 per cent [Feinstein 1972, *13*], a comment on the difficulty of measuring income in Britain before the first census of production.

The statistical thinking so far described has been about averages, 'means' as statisticians have it. The mean tells approximately where a certain number is. A desirable refinement in telling where it is would be to know how approximate the whereness was. When thinking about any number – the price of American slaves in 1860, income in Britain in 1870, Indian population in 1881, the English wheat yield around 1300 – a statistically trained person will think of a 'distribution' around the average, The average net wheat yield per unit of seed on the manors of the Bishop of Winchester in the early fourteenth century was about 3. But sometimes it was lower or higher. The spread of the distribution is exhibited in the solid bell of Figure 3. A measure of the spread of the distribution is the same 'standard deviation' mentioned above in connection with the error of an estimate. Here the standard deviation is about 1.04 bushels of wheat per bushel of seed.[2] The mean of 3.0 and the standard deviation of 1.04 serve to describe the distribution. In the special but not rare case of the 'normal' curve (a technical term, not a description of its personality) these two numbers alone describe the distribution completely.

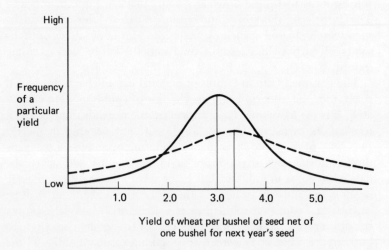

Figure 3. The standard deviation is a measure of the spread of yields around their mean

It is usually a more delicate task to measure the approximate spread of a distribution than to measure its approximate location. That is, it is harder to measure the standard deviation than the corresponding mean. In consequence the historical study of spreads, distributions, regional variability and the like tends naturally to follow after the study of locations, means and national averages. Simon Kuznets and Robert Gallman calculated American national income in the nineteenth century, before Richard Easterlin and then others attempted income by state and region [Easterlin, 1961 and Conference on Research in Income and Wealth 1960; Munyon, 1977; Field, 1978; Niemi, 1974]. During the 1970s the distribution of American income to rich and poor attracted the attention of historians previously concerned with its average size [Smolensky, 1971; Soltow, 1975; Lebergott, 1976; Williamson and Lindert 1980]. One of their findings was that twists of the income distribution have more to do with the age structure of the population than with the struggle between Labour and Capital. But the very finding shows

52

how hard it is to see beyond the true mean to the true standard deviation.

The political concerns of the 1970s were not irrelevant to the new interest in distribution. When the natural sequence from measuring the mean to measuring the variation around the mean is reversed the cause is often the pull of politics: the issues of quantification in history were fought out early in a famous debate between R. M. Hartwell and Eric Hobsbawm about the distribution of British income during the industrial revolution; this was well before anyone knew what the total income to be distributed was. The issue was felt to be too urgent to be postponed, however difficult it was to measure the spread of the income distribution. The debate continues a quarter century afterwards, gradually improving in quality as the average income figures improve [Hartwell and Engerman, 1975; O'Brien and Engerman, 1981; Williamson, 1981].

The logic of distributions has uses other than description. Since the 1950s it has influenced economic theory, and historical economists have made good use of the new theories. An instance is Paul David's argument about the mechanical reaper, which depends on a distribution of farm sizes to explain the gradualness of the adoption. Another is an argument about why farmers in the South after the American Civil War grew so much cotton. Gavin Wright and Howard Kunreuther [1975] suggest that small farmers were enticed into planting cotton, even though it was a highly variable crop, because planting cotton gave them a higher average income. They needed the high average income, regardless of its riskiness, in order to pay their rents. The notion of a 'trade off of risk for return' – that is, accepting a project with a high standard deviation so long as it also has a high average to make up for the risk – is part of the theoretical equipment of any economist. As usual, it is a piece of common sense slightly refined.

Another application of the idea of average and standard deviation explains the scattered holdings of medieval peasants. Consolidation such as occurred in modern times would have led to 13 per cent higher average output. But without the diversity of a scattered farm the peasant's income would have deviated quite far from the average fairly often: the standard deviation expressed as a ratio to the average (a statistic called the 'coefficient of variation', by the way) would have been 0.44 instead of 0.35. Look back at Figure 3, which shows the distribution for a consolidated farm as a dashed curve. Notice that the curve is pushed over to the right (its average is higher) but is spread out more (its standard deviation is also higher). The peasants could choose between scattering and consolidation, between the solid, safe-but-poor distribution and the dotted, risky-but-rich distribution. They chose the safe-but-poor one [McCloskey, 1976], scattering their land to get a more diverse and stable holding. The preference for safety first – not tradition, egalitarianism, or inheritance – explains the open fields.

The most imposing quantitative tool of the historical economist, and the one most likely to silence the literati, goes by the peculiar name of 'regression'. It amounts to no more than the drawing of a good straight line through a scatter of points. One could do the drawing with the eye, just as one could average a set of numbers with the eye. Regression merely routinises the drawing, in the way that calculating the average routinises the averaging.

The formula for a straight line connecting, say, American immigration with the American wage would be in general: immigration $= a + b$ (wage). The formula says that the amount of immigration rises by an amount b when the wage rises by one unit. (The a and b remain to be discovered.) If in 1880 the wage was low, then according to the formula the number of immigrants would also be low. If in 1881 the wage rose, then immigration would be higher. How much higher will depend on the value discovered for the slope, b. If the slope were zero, for instance, then the wage would have no effect, and immigration would *not* rise as the wage did. The wage in this case would not be reckoned a cause of immigration.

'Regression analysis' asks, what, in view of the way immigration and the wage actually behaved historically, is the best guess for the value of a and, especially, b? The question is a generalisation of the question asking for the best guess of the average of some numbers. The reason an average is not instantly calculable is that the many numbers vary around it; likewise, the reason the slope of the regression line is not instantly see-able is that the many points plotting the pairs of immigration and wage over many years vary around the line. The scatter in Figure 4 illustrates the procedure. The solid line is clearly better (the data are hypothetical). The best line according to the usual procedure is the one that makes as small as possible the vertical divergences between the line and the scattered points.[3] Any other line, such as the dashed one, would be worse.

54

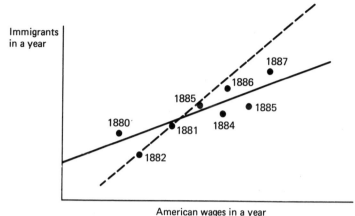

Figure 4. Regression analysis means fitting a line that is as close as possible on balance to the observed scatter

If history were co-operative it would perform the experiment on immigration and wages free of extraneous factors. History usually is not co-operative – harvest failures, wars and revolutions, lamentably rare, are the only generators of clean experiments in history. Since the experiment is not controlled, a regression of immigration on the wage all by itself would probably yield nonsense (this is why the data in the diagram are hypothetical). But the regression is easy to generalise to more than one factor influencing immigration. Instead of:

immigration $= a + b$ (wage)

you might want to use:

immigration $= a + b$ (wage) $+ c$ (cost of voyage)

It is the generalisation to more than two dimensions that makes the formal procedures better than eye-balling: you cannot eye-ball a plane through a three- or four-dimensional scatter of points. Contrariwise, only if there are second and third factors influencing immigration is regression really necessary. The additional factors serve as experimental controls, segregating the effects of cheapening transport or conditions in Europe or whatever other factors might influence immigration from the effects of the American wage.

Lowell Gallaway and Rickard K. Vedder [1971], for instance, used multivariate regression analysis on the data of American immigration from Britain, 1860–1913. They discovered from it that

America more than Britain caused the migration from Britain: a number of pull variables from the American side explain 40 per cent of the variation in emigration flows, while push variables explain only an additional 22 per cent. The rest, to 100 per cent, are explained by other variables in the equation, or by error [see Dunlevy and Gemery, 1977; Vedder and Gallaway, 1972; Thomas, 1954, 1972].

Elaborations of the idea of regression analysis travel under different names. 'Factor analysis', for instance, is a way of finding patterns in a great mass of otherwise unanalysable data for many countries or individuals, detecting clusters of behaviour. Thus Cynthia Taft Morris and Irma Adelman pursued 'Patterns of Industrialization in the Nineteenth and Early Twentieth Centuries: A Cross-Sectional Quantitative Study' [1980]. 'Spectral analysis' accomplishes the same task for one country of individual over time, detecting cycles of behaviour. Thus Larry Neal pursued a 'Cross Spectral Analysis of Atlantic Migration' [1976].

The 'econometric' model properly so called represents the limit in squeezing information out of what the past has left. It is a fitting of economic theory to the past using the most sophisticated methods for extracting the controlled effect of each of many variables. By such methods Jeremy Atack was able to show that contrary to common opinion the American South was not prevented in the middle of the nineteenth century by the small scale of its local markets from making manufactures efficiently [1985]; Philip Friedman confirmed in detail the common opinion that Europe sank itself further in depression during the 1930s by indulging in tariff wars [1978]; Michael Edelstein overturned the notion that Indian bonds in the nineteenth century, when properly corrected for risk, were worse investments than domestic British enterprise allegedly 'starved of funds' [1976, 1982]. Regression is the economist's trusty friend in this dark world and wide.

Economists are accustomed to thinking of regression as their only friend, their only method of confronting the quantitative facts of the world. They are mistaken. Scarcely realising it, they use another method at least as much, 'simulation'. Regression has its intellectual origins in biological experiment, such as studies of how rainfall affects the growth of wheat. Simulation has its origins in engineering and applied mathematics, such as studies of stresses in the Tay Bridge. Regression is curve fitting; simulation is trying things out numerically. Both are ways of submitting to the discipline of numbers, though in neither is the submission without reservation. Scientists do not 'generalize theories from collections of numbers' as is usually thought; they fit some of the world's numbers into the prevailing theories.

The importance of simulation is especially plain in historical economics. Regression is profligate with observations, and the historical economist, though diligent in acquiring the observations he has, is often hard put to acquire more. Indeed, it is not clear what 'more observations' means when the observation is, say, productivity growth in America in the nineteenth century or the effect of money growth in the Great Depression of the 1930s. The events and even the underlying patterns of behaviour that historians wish to understand are frequently unique. The uniqueness, however, does not mean that the events are beyond the clammy grip of economists and calculators. On the contrary: one can substitute carefully chosen assumptions for the data used up so quickly in the fitting of curves. That is, one can simulate.

The simplest example of simulation in economic history is 'cost/benefit analysis'. This means, of course, the careful listing of the costs and the benefits of a project, guided with a light hand by economic theory. What is being 'simulated' is the decision facing the cotton textile manufacturer contemplating the installation of ring spindles in 1900 [Sandberg, 1974] or the decision that Chicago faced in providing fresh water in the late nineteenth century [Cain, 1979]. Instead of regressing ring spindles on relative wages in Massachusetts and Lancashire or water quality on miles of sewer, the historical economist here supplies the list of possible costs and benefits, then estimates their magnitude from engineering specifications, construction expenses, profit figures, training manuals and other bits of data. The simulation needs assumptions – managers wished to maximise profits; a spinner could handle only one machine – but the assumptions are not plucked out of the air. No less than regression analysis or controlled experiment, simulation is based in fact. Just as an error in the figures used for a regression can harm the estimate, so too an error in setting out the magnitudes can harm a cost-benefit analysis [see Lazonick, 1981].

Other sorts of simulation make more demands on economic theory. For instance the method of measuring 'total factor productivity change' uses explicitly the (neoclassical) economist's theory of employment, called 'marginal productivity'. The notion is to get a measure of how well an economy used the human and material resources it had. The method was invented in the 1920s by the earliest of historical economists, G. T. Jones, a student of Alfred Marshall at Cambridge. Jones's book, published posthumously in 1933, was ignored by economists, and his method had to be re-invented in the 1950s.

The method begins simply by dividing output by an index of inputs. This is evidently what one means by 'productivity'. The theory earns its keep by providing a way to add up the inputs into one composite index. Briefly put, the way is to use the shares of an input in costs, so that for example the inputs of iron ore in producing British pig iron in the late nineteenth century are weighted at 38 per cent. The method amounts to dividing the growth of, say, pig iron into two parts: one part is fully explained, using the theory of marginal productivity, by the growing amounts of ore, coal, labour, machinery and other inputs; the other, residual, part is *not* so explained. For this reason productivity change is often called 'the residual'. It is what is left over to be explained in economic growth after the routine growth of inputs have been fully accounted for. It is what non-routine ingenuity in all its forms has contributed to our daily bread.

Historical economists have used the method of the residual intensively. Its modern reinventor, Robert Solow, used it to show that the bulk of American economic growth in the twentieth century was *not* explained by the painful accumulation of capital but by something else, in the residual – perhaps the painful accumulation of human ingenuity. His finding was wonderfully elaborated in work by Edward Denison [1962], which exhibits the skill of simulation in economics at its best. Later two historical economists pushed Solow's measure back, discovering that in the nineteenth century, before the applications of science to industry known as the second industrial revolution, the role of sheer accumulation of capital was larger [Abramovitz and David, 1973].

The method can be applied of course to single industries, and for such applications it is helpful to know that it can be measured by using the *prices* of inputs and outputs as easily as the *quantities* of inputs and output. The essential notion is that a more productive industry will use, by definition, less inputs to make a given output, and therefore will incur less costs. A more productive pig iron maker, who uses less coal and less labour per ton, can make the iron cheaper. The cheapening of pig iron relative to the prices of inputs of iron ore, labour, coal and the rest will reveal the growth of productivity just as precisely as will the rise of physical output relative to physical inputs. By exploiting this charming 'duality' between quantity and price Douglass North [1968], one of the first of the historical economists and a prolific trainer of historical economists at the University in the western state of Washington, was able to measure productivity change in ocean shipping 1600–1850. He found that it was high down to the late eighteenth century and explosive from 1814 to 1850 – even though the underlying technology of sail on wooden vessels did not change.

This is how simulation works: assume some economic model whose truth is either uncontroversial or independently testable; use the model, together with the world's facts, to discern the strength of some particular effect of interest. The simulation that makes the most demands on economic theory is the simulation of models of whole economies. The questions they address are historically unique, and quite unsuited to the repetitive requirements of regression. Who paid for the tariff on manufacturing imports in the United States before the Civil War of 1861–65? The answer is contained in the simulations of the entire American economy by Pope [1972], the first to use the method, James [1978, 1984], Pincus [1977], Baack and Ray [1983]. Who benefited in the early nineteenth century from the stop-go policies of land sales from the western domains? [Passell and Schmundt, 1971; Passell and Wright, 1972]. Was capital accumulation after the war affected by the way the Civil War was financed? [Williamson, 1974a] Who bore the costs of Britain's war against Napoleon? [Hueckel, 1973]. In each of these the workings of the economy are assumed from outside evidence to be such and such: the share of labour in agriculture is about so and so; the elasticity of demand for manufacturing is about thus and such. With the machinery in place one 'turns the crank', as the engineers put it, generating estimates of how a cause here had through a long chain an effect there.

Like the theoretical tools, then, the quantitative tools of historical economists are those of a modern doctoral-trained economist. Easy to explain in English, they are easiest to use in mathematics. Nothing in the mathematics demands that the theory be used to reach particular historical conclusions. This is by contrast with, say, the cruder forms of free-market or Marxist history. In fact, sophisticated

Marxist economic historians in the United States use modern economic theory to arrive at conclusions hostile to capitalism, though hardly agreeable to every tenet of *Capital* [Lazonick, 1981; Elbaum and Lazonick, 1984; Marglin, 1976].

Their mathematical tools make historical economists unusual among historians. Their historical materials make them unusual among economists, and promise in the long run to alter economics. Economists, it has been noted, are stubbornly present-minded. But the uses of economics in reinterpreting economic history will eventually disturb the intellectual provinciality. To a survey of the uses in economic history we now turn.

4 The Reinterpretation of American Economic History

The claim of the historical economists to have 'reinterpreted' American economic history – the word was used in the title of a collection edited by Fogel and Engerman – was only a little bold in 1971. By now it is fully justified. Another fat volume published about the same time, which also collected pieces from the major reinterpreters, declared itself to be *American Economic Growth: An Economist's History of the United States* [Davis Easterlin, Parker et al., 1972]. The piling up of historical economics since 1957 certainly does justify a reinterpretation of American economic history in the economist's way. By now numerous textbooks do so: Brownlee [1974], Gray and Peterson [1974], Niemi [1975], Temin [1975], Vedder [1976], Lee and Passell [1979], Ratner, Soltow and Sylla [1979], North, Anderson and Hill [1983], Hughes [1983] and Lebergott [1984]. Whatever their methodological approach the texts are dominated by the new findings. The *Encyclopedia of American Economic History* [1980], edited by Glenn Porter, contains a high proportion of cliometric articles. The *Bibliography of Historical Economics*, as noted earlier, contains over 4500 items. Only a few are selected here.

The economist's way of reinterpreting early colonial history, for example, used elementary counting or maybe not so elementary, such as Anderson's reckoning of colonial wealth for the late seventeenth century [1975] or Gemery's of British immigration [1980]. The first census was not taken until 1789, but before that anyway the legal records of a settled and literate community tell much. In a bicentennial effort, for example, Ball and Walton [1976] were able to reconstruct the population and wealth of Chester County, Pennsylvania, before the Revolution of 1776. Alice Hanson Jones [1980] used the inventories of goods owned by the recently deceased to paint a detailed picture of the wealth of the living in the revolutionary era. Other efforts in economic accounting have extended and corrected an older story based on pamphlets and official correspondence.

Rejoicing in a faith that the Lord will provide statistics, the economist none the less recognises that the Lord helps them who help themselves. The records of colonial trade and even the trade among the colonies themselves is retrievable in detail, showing for example that the coastal trade was large and that the triangular trade famed in older textbooks was trivial [Shepherd and Walton, 1972; Williamson and Shepherd, 1972]. Winifred Rothenberg has found that the overland trade in goods and loans was large enough to involve most colonial people in the market [1981, 1985]. Even stumbling about in the supposed statistical dark ages of the seventeenth and eighteenth centuries the historical economists have found statistics in unlikely sources. They have been keen students of the sources.

David Galenson's work on the colonial labour force is a good example. It concerns the indentured servants from which a third of the American population in 1776 had descended [1981] and the slaves on which half of the new population relied [1986]. Galenson exploited the court records of England itself and of the Chesapeake Bay region to show the economic character of indentures; and later he exploited the business records of the Royal African Company to show the equally economic character of the trade in blacks. He applied regression analysis to detect the shifts of labour demand and supply in North America and the Caribbean. He and other social and economics historians, such as Daniel Scott Smith and Russell Menard, are rewriting the history of American colonisation. This creativity of the New Colonial Historians comes from their seriousness about quantitative sources and their grasp of social theory, whether economic or sociological, theories which give fresh ways to look at the sources.

Most of the settlements on the Atlantic seaboard did not remain subjects of the Crown, sad to say, and it is around the reasons for their rebellion that some of the earliest historical economics gathered. The question was whether the taxation and restriction on colonial commerce imposed by Britain was a large burden. American mythology, prevalent even nowadays and confirmed in more grey shadings by many historians, portrays the British as mercilessly heaping duties on such vital necessities as treasonable newspapers and India tea. George III, Farmer George, is still viewed by Americans as a grasping tyrant.

In 1965, however, Robert Paul Thomas showed that the various burdens amounted not to the 10 or 20 or even 30 per cent that the revolutionary talk might suggest, but to less than 1 per cent of the average colonial income. This frightful burden in fact paid for only part of a service consumed by the colonies, namely, protection from the Indians goaded by the French. By 1763, at considerable cost to the British, the threat had been eliminated (Americans call the Seven Years War the 'French and Indian War'). But King George's American subjects showed scant gratitude. They wanted British taxpayers, less wealthy by this time than themselves, to go on paying for the bulk of imperial defence.

Thomas, in short, had turned the story on its head: like the second empire, bejewelled with India, the first British empire was in economic perspective no great burden on the colonies. Quite possibly it was a benefit; and it was very likely a burden on Britain itself. Thomas, and Philip Coelho [1973], extended the calculations to the jewel of the first empire, Jamaica. Take it as given that the quarrelsome yeomen of the mainland colonies were not profitable subjects; this might be expected. But surely one would expect that the slaves and supervisors of the Caribbean plantations would have been profitable. Surely Britain got more than it gave from Jamaica. Yet it was not so. Jamaican sugar sold in Britain at a higher price than it fetched on world markets. The owners of Jamaican plantations, being a notoriously effective lobby in Parliament, gained much from the British link; but the great British public did not. Imperialism was a subsidy for colonials.

The Thomas findings provoked comment, mainly from other historical economists refining this or that assumption in the calculations [McClelland, 1969; Reid, 1970; Walton, 1971]. The question was ideally suited to blackboard history, since it amounted to the question of who pays a tax on commerce, the oldest question in political economy and the best understood. Thomas's findings survived the scrutiny. Whatever the symbolic importance of the taxes and regulations, which could be irritants to a people unaccustomed to close governing, the economic burdens on the colonists were small.

As is common in such exercises the main contribution did not come in the detail. The contribution was to establish the order of magnitude of the burden and to compare it to a relevant standard, here the standard of colonial income in total. The burden may or may not have been a significant spark to the American Revolution [Reid, 1978]. Anyway, no amendment of the calculation could make it quantitatively large.

The revolution in transport was a later topic for reinterpretation: it was later in the history of the United States and later also in the cliometric movement. The nineteenth century saw big changes in moving corn to Chicago and people to Philadelphia, and the changes have been seen as especially American. The much-remarked 'great distances to be covered in America' were enlarged west of the Mississippi, distance added after 1800 by conquest and purchase. Yet the remark about 'great distances' is not good economics. A mile is a mile whether laid out between New York and Chicago or between London and Rome. Cheaper transport per mile was an international not an American development, speeding British coal and Argentinian beef and Australian wool as much as American wheat.

Robert Fogel's *Railroads and American Economic Growth* [1964] made the first and largest contribution, setting the terms of subsequent discussion. Paralleled in method and to some degree in conclusions by Albert Fishlow's book published about the same time, *American Railroads and the Transformation of the Antebellum Economy* [1965], Fogel's book showed more decisively than any previous work the uses of economics in history.

The point of Fogel's work is simple. It is that railways were cheaper than other modes, but not so much cheaper that the nation was enormously enriched by the cheapening. This is surprising. According to the traditional thinking, emphasised by all who had looked into the matter and re-emphasised by the great economists Joseph Schumpeter and W. W. Rostow, the railway was the dominant machine of the nineteenth century, the maker and enricher of nations. Especially it was the enricher of the American nation, with its 'great distances'.

The details of Fogel's answer are worth knowing. If the railway was dominant in American economic growth, said Fogel, one might say it was 'indispensable' (in his earliest work on the subject, in fact, he started by assuming as everyone else did that it *was* indispensable). That is to say, had the railway been dispensed with the course of American economic history would have been very different. Now of course no one could deny that an America without railways would have been different in geography. A landlocked place like Denver, sitting on the edge of the Rockies in Colorado, would have stagnated as a tiny cattle town without the railway; a riverine place like St. Louis, as the main city on the northern Mississippi, would have grown even larger. It is this sort of mental experiment that convinced people that of course the railway was important.

But Fogel asked whether the nation without railways would have been much richer *on the whole,* taking together the diminished Denver and the enlarged St. Louis. It is, again, a swings-and-roundabouts question. He answered it by noting that the resources unused in Denver without the railway would not have evaporated. Denver is not the only place for people and horses and iron. They would have found employment elsewhere, including St. Louis. To look at the point the other way around, the nation as a whole after the railway did not gain every dollar of the income earned in Denver *net.* The expansion of Denver took resources from the rest of the nation – for instance, from St. Louis. The resources were merely relocated by the settlement of Denver; they were not created free, out of nothing.

The next step is to observe that if wheat, say, is produced in both St. Louis and Denver, and if there is no tendency for investment to move from one to the other, then the growing of wheat must be equally profitable in both places. This is mere common sense. Sensible investors will shift their funds until the equality is true: the net profitability of wheat growing must be the same in the two places, or else the wheat growing moves. But Denver's profitability must bear a high cost of transport, since it is further from markets. Its 'raw' (or gross) profitability, so to speak, must therefore be initially higher. If one could magically eliminate Denver's disadvantages in location the nation would take advantage of the higher raw profitability, moving resources to Denver. The nation would of course be delighted to earn the higher profit. But the nation cannot earn it without some magic: Denver is badly located, far from consuming centres.

The magic comes from the railway. The railway brought down the extra cost of transport that Denver had to bear. The difference in raw profitability is what the nation gains if it can shift resources profitably to Denver. But the difference in profitability is, for the reason just given, *exactly the extra cost of transporting the wheat from Denver.* If one measures the fall in transport costs, therefore, one is measuring the rise in national income caused by the coming of the railway to Denver.[4]

Fogel then asked how much it would have cost nationally to

transport the wheat and other goods in 1890 had the railway never been invented. In such a case, plainly, the goods would have had to go by water or road if they went at all. The water or road must have been dearer than the railway, or else the goods would actually have gone by water or road anyway. Turning it around, then, the question of dispensability reduces to the question of how much cheaper the railway was than the next best alternative. The 'social saving', as Fogel called it, can be measured if the cost of alternatives – canals and roads – can be compared with the railways.

Fogel's argument thus far uses merely the refined common sense of economic theory. One could have discovered so much by reading Schumpeter and Rostow, then sitting in a dark room and thinking quietly, especially if one had a fertile brain and a doctorate in economics (the book was in fact Fogel's doctoral thesis at Johns Hopkins University, once a centre for historical economics).

Most of Fogel's book, though, is devoted to the next step. He proceeds to calculate the actual cost in 1890 of canals and roads compared with railways, going so far as to imagine in detail the canals that might have been built had the railway not existed. As noted above, there is little of a strictly 'econometric' character in this; here Fogel, like most historical economists, wants merely to make a defensible guess at one or two numbers, and for this purpose needs sophisticated economic theory more than sophisticated statistical theory.

Fogel concludes that the social saving was no more than a few per cent of national income, the economic growth of only a year or two. He arranges his guessing, furthermore, to give if anything an exaggerated estimate. When faced with uncertain choices between two numbers in the calculation, such as a high or low estimate of the length of time in winter that canals were frozen, unable to carry freight, he picks the number that biases the case against himself: here, the lower figure. And he forces his hypothetical system of canals to carry freight over the same routes and in the same volumes as the actual railways. A canal system would in fact have resulted in a different geography of growing and eating, better suited to water than to rail: Denver would have been smaller, St. Louis bigger. Forcing the canals to deal with the wrong geography – forcing canals to bring wheat from the dry plateau of eastern Colorado – will exaggerate their cost relative to railways and will lead again to an overestimate, if anything, of the saving to be had from railways.

Fogel's estimate, to use a word increasingly popular in applied statistics, is 'robust' to possible errors. Robust and small.

Viewed from economics the smallness of the social saving is not very surprising. To show that it is not, one can use the same argument invented for assessing the burden of the eighteenth-century empire [e.g. McClelland, 1969]. Fogel's game is won as soon as the thinking in the dark room has brought the question around to the cost of transport, because transport does not account for an overwhelmingly large share of national income – only 10 per cent or so. To be sure, if transport were literally shut down the figure would be irrelevant, because some remnant of transport is literally 'essential'. One could hardly say that if people were shot for carrying their tomatoes across the street, or walking to school, the loss to national income would be only 10 per cent. But short of such an extreme there are substitutes for transport, such as the closing down of Denver; and certainly there are substitutes for railways, such as canals.

In a world of substitutes the size of the industry is what governs its importance. A 50 per cent less efficient transport industry is a bad thing, but after all it would affect only 10 per cent of national income. The railways were in fact about 50 per cent cheaper than canals on competing routes. Roughly half of all the traffic went by canal, river, or road even after the railway (you had to get the stuff to the railway station; and coal, salt, sand and the like continued to be transported cheaply if slowly by barge).

The upshot is a product of three terms: transport was only 10 per cent of national income; only half of it was affected at all by the railway; and on this half the saving was about 50 per cent. The social saving therefore is about (0.10) $(1/2)$ $(0.50) = 0.025$, or 2.5 per cent of national income. This is in fact the order of magnitude of Fogel's more careful estimate made directly from the primary sources.

The reasonableness of Fogel's estimate notwithstanding, it provoked great controversy [David, 1969; McClelland, 1980; O'Brien, 1977; Fremdling, 1977]. Historians were chiefly alarmed by the 'counterfactual' method discussed earlier. Economists were alarmed by what they regarded as misleading assumptions in Fogel's chain of argument. Their alarm was probably unnecessary, though it will be a while before the dust settles entirely. If the canals could have handled the additional traffic only at much greater expense, for example, the assumption that the canal rates actually observed during 1890 (in a world with extensive railways taking much of the traffic) would be too low. The social savings would be under-instead of over-estimated. Fogel, however, made allowances for this. Again, if the coming of Denver yielded economies of scale, it would no longer be a matter of indifference whether resources were located in Denver or St. Louis. Yet we have seen that arguments from economies of scale need careful handling, and are not to be brought down casually as *dei ex machina*. The problem here is that the argument is asymmetrical: it forgets that economies of scale could just as plausibly have arisen from the great expansion of St. Louis in a watery world.

All in all the criticisms of Fogel's calculations have an insubstantial air. Fogel might well have replied with Newton and Hume, *Hypotheses non fingo,* which is to say that he might well have disregarded 'critics of his theory . . . who merely point out that it conflicts with this or that speculative hypothesis; criticism must take the form of bringing forward facts which conflict with the theory' [Passmore, 1980, 47]. In his presidential address to the American Economic History Association in 1978 he made essentially this reply [Fogel, 1979].

Nearly uniquely, Jeffrey Williamson brought forward facts rather than possibilities against Fogel, though as we have seen his argument has frailties of its own (to which he too might make the Newtonian reply [Williamson, 1974]). For the rest one would have to judge that twenty years after the battle Fogel remains in possession of the field.

The outcomes of this first full-scale battle among the historical economists themselves were substantive and methodological. In substance, Fogel's conclusion served to weaken the already tottering edifice of W. W. Rostow's stage theory. This was its main purpose, as it was of Fishlow's book and many other pieces of historical economics: Rostow's contribution was in the end to stimulate fruitful criticism (a noble accomplishment). Fogel's conclusion makes it hard to claim for railways or other 'infrastructure' vague but immense 'multiplier effect' (the jargon is routinely misunderstood in this connection). Students of economic development do not read history (unless they chance to write it: [Rostow, 1960; Lewis, 1970; Kelley and Williamson, 1974; Latham, 1978; Heston and Kumar 1983]) and therefore take their opinions of how the rich nations accomplished the trick from the cinema and the newspaper. The cinema and the newspaper make much of romantic pieces of equipment like the Iron Horse. Fogel's conclusion would set them straight. The conclusion was reinforced by studies of passenger traffic and of other transport in nineteenth century America [Walton and Boyd, 1972; Mak, Haites and Walton, 1975]. And it was reinforced by studies of railways in other countries. The conclusion is that in a well-watered plain, such as the American Midwest, railways are desirable but not indispensable. They were not the engine for America's take-off into self-sustained growth.

But the main outcomes of the controversy over Fogel's work were methodological, imparting a spin to historical economics. For one thing, Fogel made counterfactuals a respectable figure of speech in economic history, a way of talking not limited to books on the philosophy of history. For another, he made the rhetoric of the argument *a fortiori* central to the field. The book consists of an attempt to find the 'least upper bound' (a term from mathematics) on the benefit from railways. If the upper bound is small *a fortiori* the true effect is small. He draws on the argument very frequently [for instance, on pp. *20, 23, 28, 45, 47*], biasing the case against himself. The argument is widely used in our culture: it is a 'common topic', or usual figure of speech. Rogue Riderhood in *Our Mutual Friend,* for instance, used it in attempting to frame Gaffer Hexam by perjured affidavit: 'He says to me, "Rogue Riderhood, you are a man in a dozen" – I think he said in a score, but of that I am not positive, so take the lower figure, for precious be the obligation of an Alfred David.'

Fogel's use of this figure of speech has led many research students to take up careers of under- and overestimating things. The usual rhetoric of history in such matters (and of economics, though less prominently displayed) demands 'accuracy'. An estimate of the population of fifth-century Athens must be 'accurate'; a description of the American economy as competitive is to be judged for 'accuracy'. Yet a physicist would note that the word is meaningless without bounds on the error; and a literary critic would note that the accuracy necessary to the argument depends on the conversational context. There is no absolute sense of 'accuracy', as Oskar Morgenstern once argued to economists in his neglected classic, *On the Accuracy of Economic Observations* [1963].

Fogel's method attracted converts because it responded to such remarks. Neither conventional econometrics nor conventional historical methods do. The young scholar adopting Fogel's rhetoric could now make an estimate that would bear on a real conversation of scholarship. By recognising that 'accuracy' depends on how much accuracy is needed to persuade he could advance the conversation, building a case on necessarily 'inaccurate' estimates (for example, small but overstated estimates of something it is desired to prove small). No wonder Fogel's book dazzled the young.

Above all, Fogel created an audience for the kind of book he had written. He required a reader that was in 1964 nearly a contradiction in terms, one who was both a historically interested economist and an economically sophisticated historian. Only such a composite could appreciate the argument of his book to the full. Its intellectual success in time created many such readers, these historical economists. Fogel was an orator setting up his platform in Hyde Park, gathering after a while a crowd capable of appreciating his speech (and a regular band of hecklers, too), and sending out disciples to use his lawyerly, technical and argumentative style.

The railways were more than a means of transport. Investment in American railways took much of national savings, and by its jagged expansion caused – or at least vigorously expressed – many of the booms and busts from the 1840s to the 1890s [Neal, 1969; Dick, 1974]. In his study of the second of these booms, during which the railways spread to the rich agriculture of Illinois and Iowa, Fishlow [1965] had shown that the investment in railways came from local sources, the people to be benefited. By this he contradicted the many economists who believed that a project with widespread beneficiaries would always require central co-ordination. And he showed, contradicting historians, that the investment came *after* settlement, not before: there was no building ahead of demand. In later work Fishlow showed that the railway system continued to improve rapidly, saving as much by the perfection of locomotives and airbreaks as it had saved over canals and roads on its introduction [Fishlow, 1966]. The case was similar in other industries, which have been found to have achieved as much when growing to maturity as during their heroic infancies.

Manufacturing industry, except as freight and as suppliers of railways, has received less attention from American historical economists [Uselding, 1980]. The British tradition of economic history has been to treat each sort of manufacturing as a character in a many-charactered Iliad of ingenuity. The American tradition has been to downplay manufacturing, and to treat agriculture as a lone

Odysseus voyaging from forest to forge and from prairie to corn-belt. Transport and manufacturing are treated as supporting characters in a mainly bucolic drama. The first study of a manufacturing industry by a historical economist is still one of the best, Paul McGouldrick's *New England Textiles in the Nineteenth Century: Profits and Investment* [1968]. The cotton textile industry, as the first big industry to use factories, has attracted much attention [Nickless, 1979; Zevin, 1971; Wright, 1979; McHugh, 1984]. The iron industry, though much smaller than cotton, has simple inputs and an apparently important output; this makes it ideal for quantitative study [Temin, 1969; Fogel and Engerman, 1969]. More recently the historical economists have used the early censuses of production to tell how other industries grew, and why in some places they did not [Atack, 1985; Weiss, Bateman and Foust, 1971; Sokoloff, 1984a, b].

American industry used somewhat different techniques from British industry: flimsier rails on railways, higher pressures in steam engines [Temin, 1966a], and more elaborate machinery for shaping wood [Ames and Rosenberg, 1968]. The contrast was emphasised in a book written in 1962 by J. H. Habakkuk, *American and British Technology in the Nineteenth Century,* one of the handful of recent works by a non-economist to have had much influence among historical economists (another is Alfred Chandler's brilliant *The Visible Hand,* on the rise of the corporation). Habakkuk's theme, as elaborated for instance in Paul David's book, *Technological Change and Economic Growth* [1975], was that technological change is influenced by the economic environment. Habakkuk emphasised especially the labour-saving character of American practice.

A steady stream of ingenious and learned essays by historical economists has attempted to square and resquare the argument with the evidence [Uselding and Juba, 1973; Harley, 1974; Field, 1983;]. These taught in detail what had been learned early in the conversation from Temin [1966b] and Fogel [1967]: that a two-input view, contrasting Labour with Capital, was rather too simple for the case. Relative 'scarcity of labour' was only one of the peculiarities of the new world.

Its chief peculiarity, the worm in the apple, was a seventeenth-century solution to the scarcity of labour, black slavery, abolished only in 1863 at the cost of a great civil war, leaving a mark on American society not yet wholly cleansed. This was again an agricultural matter. Though slavery was by no means inconsistent with urban and manufacturing life [Goldin, 1976; Bateman, Foust and Weiss, 1975], it did encourage especially the growing of cotton, the world supply of which came to be chiefly American [Parker (ed.), 1970; Wright, 1978].

The American fascination with the South and its peculiar institution is comparable to the British fascination with Lancashire and its satanic mills. Hundreds of economic articles and books have been written on it since 1958. One of the two inaugural pieces of historical economics published in that year (the other was Hughes and Reiter, 1958), a model for later work, was Alfred Conrad and John Meyer's 'The Economics of Slavery in the Antebellum South' [1958]. Written in the tough-minded style of modern economics by two assistant professors of economics at Harvard, it made at once the most important point: that slaves were after all machines, a form of capital. The economic theory of capital, therefore, could apply. The peculiar institution required a peculiar metaphor.

If one accepts the metaphor that slaves were machines, bought and used as capital on markets wholly capitalistic, and used to make the raw material of the first industrial revolution, the revisions following Conrad and Meyer seem less startling than they seemed at the time. For instance, in 1974 Stanley Engerman and that same Robert Fogel discovered that slaves were not wretchedly fed or housed or otherwise badly treated by comparison with free workers in the North. The assertion was instantly contradicted by other historical economists [David et al., 1976], whose unrestrained attacks on Fogel, Engerman and their students spoilt the conversation for a time. But the Fogel and Engerman position has been at length mostly vindicated. Looked at coolly the relatively mild treatment of slaves (if not of Fogel and Engerman) is not surprising. A prime-age field hand was expensive, costing in 1860 about five times the average annual earnings of a free worker. A farmer does not buy such an expensive machine in order to kick and starve it.

Again, slavery was found to be profitable, in two senses. The buying and using of a slave earned normal returns [Conrad and Meyer, 1958]; and the raising of slaves earned profits which increased over the decades of slavery's expansion [Yasuba, 1961]. Noel Butlin [1971] criticised all this early on. But with the machine metaphor in mind none of it is very surprising [Engerman, 1973]. Machines with a good market would always earn normal returns (if they did not, their price in the market would change); and the expansion of slavery showed that making more machines was a profitable undertaking.

Slavery, finally and most controversially, was found by Fogel and Engerman to be in a narrow sense efficient: not moral or good for the slaves or desirable in other ways; but yielding a great deal of cotton and corn for each hour worked and acre of land ploughed – and not only in cotton [Schmitz, 1977]. Southerners died fighting in large numbers to protect their machines (or, more exactly, the machines of the small minority of southerners who owned slaves at all). The machines were worth it: 'the wealth piled up by the bondsman's two hundred and fifty years of unrequited toil'. If the slave machines were in fact as inefficient as Northern abolitionists and Southern sentimentalists believed at the time it would be hard to understand why the South was impelled to break with the Union.

The resulting Civil War of 1861–65 was absolutely the bloodiest and relatively the costliest in American history. It too attracted early attention from historical economists [Andreano, 1967], who concluded against the orthodoxy erected by Charles Beard fifty years earlier that the war was not a spur to industrialisation [Engerman, 1966]. The costliness of the war affected the budget of the federal government well after peace was declared, affecting in turn the savings of Americans [Williamson, 1974a]. One clear result of the war was a sharp drop in the agricultural output of the South, even after repairing the damage from battle (almost all Southern). Inevitably the discussion of the effects of the war became entangled in the bitter dispute during the 1970s over the efficiency of slavery [Goldin and Lewis, 1975; Temin, 1976a]. If slavery was efficient there was no wonder that productivity declined when it was abolished; if it was inefficient, however, as the critics of Fogel and Engerman wished, the decline in productivity had to be explained another way.

One way to explain it, and to explain the sluggish economic performance of the South for decades after the war, was to point to a deceleration in the demand for cotton worldwide [Wright, 1978]; or to certain imperfections in the post-bellum market place, such as an over-emphasis on cotton growing to pay the rent [Wright and Kunreuther, 1975] or a re-enslavement of blacks by powerful country stores [Ransom and Sutch, 1977]. Other writers, though, accepted implicitly the economic efficiency of slavery, and marshalled evidence for the smooth and efficient functioning of markets after its abolition. The debate centred on sharecropping, an insti-

73

tution long blamed for bad Southern performance but emerging from the work of historical economists as 'an understandable market response' to the break-up of gang labour [Reid, 1973; DeCanio, 1974; Higgs, 1977; Alston and Higgs, 1982].

The combatants wore uniforms known from other battles, especially the battle between Chicago economics ('monetarism', roughly) and the rest of the world. The distinction between 'monetarists' and regular folk is not as crude in historical economics as it is in literal politics, and one must not suppose:

> That every history boy or gal
> That's borne into the books alive
> Is Labourite or Liberal
> Or else a little Conservative.

Some of the heat comes from politics; yet there is much cool light shed by politics, too, as there has been by serious Marxist history recently in Britain. On the Chicago side, for example, Reid and Higgs and others would agree that the substantial book by Ransom and Sutch, *One Kind of Freedom: The Economic Consequences of Emancipation,* which painted a picture of debt peonage replacing slavery, had at least raised the level of the debate. And from the other side, David and Temin begin their hostile reviews of *Time on the Cross* by affirming with evident warmth that it is 'an ambitious and imposing book' [David *et al., 33, 165*]; the very length of some of the reviews (reaching 75 pages in print, bizarre even by the disputatious standards of economics) testifies to an underlying admiration for the achievement.

The ideological divisions in historical economics, then, should not be overdrawn. But it would be naïve to pretend, as does the scientistic rhetoric of economics and history, that there is nothing at stake. Usually what is at stake is optimism or pessimism about the working of the market.

The battle has been fought on many fronts. The emancipation of slaves, and of women, and the immigration of poor people from Alabama, and from Poland, left these groups nonetheless with lower wages than some. The question is whether their lower wages are to be explained by sheer discrimination, which is a failure of the market to work, or by productivity, which is how it works. The question is well suited to regression analysis, and many straight lines have been fitted to many sets of data in answering it. The optimistic, Chicago side argues that lower wages are explained by productivity [Higgs, 1971b; McGouldrick and Tannen, 1977; Klingaman, Vedder and Gallaway, 1978]; the pessimists reply that productivity is itself a reflex of discriminatory institutions, such as education and training [Hannon, 1982; Margo, 1984].

The Chicago quarrel grows most heated, of course, in matters monetary. Milton Friedman, with Anna Jacobson Schwartz (herself among the pioneers of the historical economics of Britain), wrote the seminal work, *A Monetary History of the United States, 1867–1960* [1963]. The core of the book treats the Great Depression of the 1930s as a consequence of mishandled monetary policy. Like the Fogel and Engerman book on slavery, it was met by anti-Chicago fury [Temin, 1976b; Brunner (ed.), 1981], but not before it had won a place for monetarism. Friedman and Schwartz were long-time members of the National Bureau of Economic Research in New York, which practised historical economics before it was invented. They were able therefore to bring into the present-minded debates of the 1960s the prestige of Historical Facts. The effect on otherwise ahistorical economists was striking. Economists who believed themselves quite exempt from any historical influence found themselves slaves to it.

Even monetary history, however, can be written in an ideologically unpredictable way. Hugh Rockoff's elucidation of the lightly regulated banking systems during the 1840s and 1850s, for instance, de-emphasised the role of money, though Rockoff was from Chicago [1974]. Peter Temin's book on *The Jacksonian Economy* [1969] hitched it all to money, though he became the chief torturer of Friedman and Schwartz (and was to become a victim of torture in turn). It is not obvious what politics Richard Sylla espouses in his many penetrating contributions to the history of banking and money in the Atlantic economy [1969, 1976]: so too Lance Davis' pioneering studies of the national investment market [1965] or Alan Olmstead's study of *New York City Mutual Savings Banks, 1819–1961* [1976] or Eugene White's of *Regulation and Reform of the American Banking System, 1900–1929* [1983]. Even the survey article by the arch-monetarists Michael Bordo and Anna Schwartz [1977] is notable for its steady tone and catholicity of treatment. And everyone admits that the Great Depression itself, the central event in modern macroeconomics, has not yet been fully explained [Mercer and Morgan, 1972]. It is no wonder that the economic past attracts ideological interest. Yet the ideology has been more a stimulus to the asking of questions than a determinant of the answers.

Most features of the American economic past have attracted the attention of historical economists, often using the latest insights of economic theory and improving the theory by its use. The tariff, about which politics swirled for most of American history, was the subject of the earliest applications of the theory of public choice [Pincus, 1977; Baack and Ray, 1983] and of general equilibrium models [Pope, 1972; Passell and Schmundt, 1971; James, 1978]. Terry Anderson and P. J. Hill [1975], Gary Libecap [1978, 1984], Joseph Reid and others have applied the emerging economics of property rights and transactions costs to American problems. The economics of immigration, and of other demographic events, has been used and improved in American economic history [Neal and Uselding, 1972]. The economics of law and regulation has a prosperous historical annex [Ulen, 1980]. The economic history of women may eventually force neoclassical economics to adopt a more sensible model of the household [Goldin, 1984; Rotella, 1980]. So it goes.

And so it has gone, proliferating over the journals of economics and economic history, filling a small library of books. Can a nation's economic history be reinterpreted using economics? Yes, of course it can.

5 Pax Cliometrica

In this way historical economics won the West. While winning the United States, however, it was sending armies elsewhere, as Duke William's cousins conquered Apulia and Sicily, too. A survey of many thousands of writings cannot be complete. But to conclude with a rapid tour of the outposts, a mere selective list of who has done or is doing what will perhaps make one point clear: that historical economics can reinterpret histories other than the American. To some degree it already has, which will be news to many in its home. Like most national histories, American economic history is provincial, and its practitioners are mostly unaware that historical economics thrives also in such climes as Canada, Britain, Japan, Italy and far Australia fair.

Canadian economics in the 1950s had not drifted so far from history as had the economics of its bigger and more novelty-ridden neighbour. In Canada economics determines national identity, and is too important to be left to economists. The important question – can a long, thin country survive next to a big, fat one? – has been asked in mainly economic terms. Since the answer must be historical, Canada had its own stream of historical economists before the name, from the 1940s especially in the Toronto School of Harold Innis.

But in other ways the rise of historical economics in Canada resembled its rise in the United States: in contrast to Britain, research students in economics were required to attend long courses of lectures, in which they acquired technical economics at a high level; no departments of economic history existed to protect students from the techniques; Canadians even more than Americans were disproportionately represented in the ranks of technically trained economists in the 1950s and 1960s; and just as the United States took full advantage of the diaspora of intellectuals from Europe, so too for a time in the 1960s and early 1970s Canada took advantage of the international mobility of scholars (Donald Paterson of the University of British Columbia is a Scot; Robert Allen of British

Columbia, C. K. Harley of Western Ontario, and Robert Ankli of the University of Guelph are Americans). More even than American economic history, Canadian economic history is economic and statistical. A random sample of a large literature would be: Marr and Paterson [1980–a textbook]; Dick [1977 – a bibliography]; and a few themes: Chambers and Gordon [1966]; Lewis and McInnis [1980]; Patterson and Wilen [1977]; Shearer and Clark [1984]; George and Oksanen [1980]; Pacquet and Wallot [1972]; Carlos [1981]; Dick [1980]; McInnis [1977].

The British case was quite different. The invasion of historical economics was stoutly resisted until the end of the 1960s, and even now can excite harrumphing in some quarters. Though thinnish, the stream of precursors was bright and long, as might be expected from the place that invented economics. In the early nineteenth century Thorold Rogers could be found collecting wage indexes for earlier centuries. Until the 1950s and its technical explosion the British economic historians kept current in economics: J. H. Clapham practised economics as it was known in the 1920s, and contributed significantly to it. In 1933 as we saw, another student of Marshall, and of Clapham, G. T. Jones, invented productivity measurement in its modern form, though by the 1950s the economists were paying so little attention to historical writing that the measure had to be reinvented. T. S. Ashton, the holder of the chair at the London School of Economics, recast eighteenth-century British history in an economic mould. R. M. Hartwell (an Australian expatriate) and H. J. Habakkuk at Oxford applied economic common sense to industrialisation and landowning, and encouraged their students to learn more mathematics than they had done.

The most explicitly economic of British economic history, however, came from economists and foreigners. The economists were national income accountants, largely at Cambridge, extending their series back into the pre-war darkness; or polymaths like Brinley Thomas, Alec Cairncross, and R. C. O. Matthews, writing in the 1950s brilliant pieces of economic history while deeply engaged in work on more recent times. Before 1970 full-fledged economic research by a full-time economic historian in Britain, such as Alec Ford's *The Gold Standard* [1962], was rare, though if any field kept up with scholarly standards in economics it was monetary history. As noted above, the foreigners, as foreigners do, did the work the British would not, such as the street-sweeping tasks of constructing the basic series, especially of foreign trade. And Americans led in interpretive applications of economics to British economic history, beginning with Rostow in the 1940s and continuing with studies of Britain by some of the pioneers of historical economics gathered in the early 1960s at Purdue University: J. R. T. Hughes [1960], Lance Davis, Edward Ames, Nathan Rosenberg and M. June Flanders (the monument to their sojourn is *Purdue Faculty Papers in Economic History* [1967]).

The issue in British history that attracted the most interest in the late 1960s and early 1970s was entrepreneurial failure. Did Victorian Britain fail? Economists were then concerned (as they sometimes are) with the nature and causes of the wealth of nations. At the Harvard Business School an influential school had grown up that identified the crucial factor as entrepreneurship. British historians for the most part followed contemporary journalists in believing that something had gone wrong in the late nineteenth century. 'Entrepreneurship' was a convenient vessel for such beliefs.

The issue mattered because the late Victorian economy was the archetype of capitalism. In studies during the 1930s of the iron and steel industry Duncan Burn had concluded that the managers had failed from the 1870s onwards; Burn's findings, with consular reports and other bits of evidence, were used in the 1950s and 1960s by David Landes and Derek Aldcroft among others to blame Britain's sluggish growth and declining markets on entrepreneurial failure. The indictment was embraced by enemies of capitalism and by its less optimistic friends.

The defence was long in coming, stated most plainly in a conference held at Harvard University in 1970 and in the volume of papers and discussion forthcoming from it [McCloskey (ed.), 1971]. It was made chiefly by Americans, who had no shameful sense of British failure and had at any rate the economic training to make the case.

The strategy of the defence was straightforward, namely, to compare actual productivity in Britain with productivity abroad, especially productivity in Germany and the United States, as the two nations said to have exceeded Victorian Britain in vigour. The national comparisons, and the comparisons in particular industries such as iron and steel, turned out to be not especially damning to Britain [McCloskey, 1970, 1981; Floud, 1976]. Another and equivalent test was to examine the rapidity with which British businessmen adopted innovations. Again the standard was comparative, asking whether the speed of adoption fell irrationally far behind American and German rates. In a variety of industries the death of British business vigour proved to have been exaggerated [Harley, 1971; Sandberg, 1974; McCloskey, 1973; Lindert and Trace, 1971]. And Michael Edelstein showed in a series of studies that the centre-piece of Victorian capitalism, its capital market, worked reasonably well, too [1976, 1982].

There is nothing in the method that forces such results, as became apparent in the drizzle of amending criticism from other historical economists [Kennedy, 1974; Allen, 1979; Lazonick, 1981; Webb, 1980]. The main point of the critics was that the revisionists had overlooked 'dynamic' effects. The word 'dynamic' is notoriously vague in economics: often it is used as a synonym for my (good) model as against your (static) one. When the critics got down to cases they mentioned the second-round effects on variables such as invest-ment and the alleged failures in Britain to change institutions. But no one has ventured a serious quantitative estimate of these. The amendments, in other words, left the order of magnitudes un-changed. Most economists would agree that the magnitude of 'failure', if any, was small. At least it was small by the standards of the *1066-and-All-That* history once prevalent, still popular among non-economists: that America (with Germany in support) became Top Nation, and British economic history came to an end.

The studies of entrepreneurship were the first of a broader set of industrial histories, taking up in economic style the strongest tradi-tion in British economic history. Charles K. Hyde's study of the iron and steel industry in the eighteenth century [1977], C. K. Harley's ongoing study of British shipping and shipbuilding in the age of steel [1971 and others], William Hausman's work on coal in the eight-eenth century [1984], and John Lyons' on cotton textiles [1977] are typical in their use of economic reasoning, and typical too in that all the authors are North Americans. The chief historical economist of English railways, Gary Hawke [1970], is a New Zealander; as is that of the steam engine, Nicholas von Tunzelmann [1978]. Of course, the first industrial nation attracts special interest abroad, as for similar reasons does the home of Newton and Darwin and the cradle of free institutions. Foreign students of British intellectual and poli-tical history are numerous. But there are few fields of British history in which the contribution of foreigners has been so large as in nineteenth-century economic history.

All this is not to say that historical economics is unknown from British hands. Roderick Floud was involved in the controversy over entrepreneurship, and has now shifted to the demographic dimension of economic history; Nicholas Crafts has remade the statistics of the industrial revolution [1983]; James Foreman-Peck has re-examined economically the history of the motor industry [1979]; S. R. H. Jones has worked on smaller scale industries early in the industrial revolution [1973]; Mark Thomas has seen the Edwardian economy through economic eyes [1985]; in a series of brilliant studies Leslie Hannah has brought business and economic history together for the century past; and so forth. The point is merely that like the exchange of coal and wheat since the 1840s a free international trade in ideas obtains. In a recent collection on *The Economics of the Industrial Revolution,* mainly focused on Britain [Mokyr, 1985], under half the contributors are British, the rest foreign.

The free trade in ideas has its usual results in range of product. Peter Lindert [1980] and Jeffrey Williamson have collaborated to explore inequality since the seventeenth century; a group at the London Business School has produced statistics of the money supply. The Poor Law new and old has been the subject of economic studies by Easton [1978], Boyer [1985], and MacKinnon [1986] going beyond administrative history. The economics of enclosure has been a matter of dispute [McCloskey, 1975; Allen, 1982]. The economics of imperialism has been studied closely [Davis and Huttenbach, 1982]. The causes of the Great Slump between the wars have received much attention from historical economists, as much for its sharp implications for policy nowadays as for its historical interest [Moggridge, 1962; Benjamin and Kochin, 1979; Howson, 1975; Eichengreen, 1981; Eichengreen and Sachs, 1985]. And so forth. The historical economics of Britain has grown well beyond what is possible to survey in a few pages. An attempt to synthesise the period since 1700 was edited in 1981 by Floud and McCloskey.

Historical economics is not an exclusively Anglo-American subject. A survey must be desperately brief. Most Western European countries contain a vigorous minority of historical economists, and American work also on European subjects is substantial. There is work on Ireland [Ó Gráda, 1975; Mokyr, 1983]; on Italy [Fenoaltea, 1969 and forthcoming; Toniolo, 1977; Cohen, 1979; Rapp, 1976]; on Scandanavia [Jonung, 1983; Sandberg, 1979;

Jorberg and Bengtsson, 1975]; on Spain [Totella-Casares, 1975; Flynn, 1975]. This is a mere sampling, and not random at that. Scholars resident in Germany are reviving a tradition of applied economics damaged by the Second World War, and some have turned their techniques on historical questions [Hoffman, 1965; Dumke, 1977; Fremdling, 1977; Tilly, 1982]. Germany, Austria and Hungary have been the subjects of much historical economics by North American scholars [Komlos, 1983a, b; Rudolph, 1983; Webb, 1984; Haines, 1979; Good, 1984; Eddie, 1977; Neuberger and Stokes, 1974].

The Low Countries have a vigorous tradition of modern quantitative economics, and corresponding strength in historical economics [Mokyr, 1976; de Vries, 1978; Bos, 1979; De Meere, 1979]. Belgium stands between Holland and France in this as in certain other respects [Mendels, 1972]. France appears to have its mind on higher matters than supply and demand. It has nourished no more than a handful of important economists since the Second World War because French economics is still largely controlled by professors trained not in mathematics but in law. There is in France no tradition of modern economics to be bent to history. Except for a brilliant tradition of national income measurement [e.g. Toutain] the historical economics of France is therefore Anglophone [Kindleberger, 1964; Hohenberg, 1972; Grantham, 1975, 1980; Roehl, 1976; O'Brien and Keyder, 1978; Eichengreen, 1982; Weir, 1984].

The Western Europeans overseas have their historical economists, in Latin America [Coatsworth, 1981; Leff, 1968; Neuhaus (ed.), 1979] and in the Antipodes [Butlin, 1964; 1984; Forster (ed.), 1970; McLean, 1973; Barnard, Butlin and Pincus, 1982; Pope, 1976; Haig and Cain, 1983; Shlomowitz, 1979]. The only limitations are the number of graduates in neoclassical (or if you wish, bourgeois) economics, the number of academic positions devoted to the economic past, and the existence of alternative traditions in economic history: it is a matter of supply and demand.

Cliometrics is spoken, too, in and about Japan [Rosovsky, 1961; Yamamura, 1974; 1976, 1978; Kelley and Williamson, 1974; Patrick (ed), 1976; Yasuba, 1976; Mosk, 1978; Yamamura and Hanley, 1978; Saxonhouse, 1978]. The literature on China is thus far written entirely by the barbarians [Perkins, 1969; Rawski, 1980; Brandt, 1985]. Africa has attracted a little cliometric attention [Hogendorn, 1979; Lewis, 1970; Gemery and Hogendorn, 1974, 1979; Bean and

Thomas, 1974]; Southeast Asia a little, too [Feeny, 1979]; and South Asia a lot [Morris, 1965, 1983; McAlpin, 1983a, b; Kumar and Desai, (eds), 1983; Latham, 1978; Heston and Kumar, 1983].

In Russia and the Warsaw Pact the received view on such matters is too powerful to permit more than quantification without theory, especially when the history is recent. This is a pity, because Marx and Engels have a claim to being part of the thin bright stream of proto-cliometricians. They certainly contributed heavily to its customs of tabulation-cum-disputation. Again foreigners are left to do the work [Gregory, 1974, 1984; Spechler, 1980; Carstensen, 1984].

The 'unavailability of data' alleged to characterise the dark ages before 1948, which is the main thought that most economists have about economic history, is no barrier to using economics. True, historical economics is still not widely practised on medieval subjects [North and Thomas, 1973; Fenoaltea, 1984; Roehl, 1972; McCloskey, 1976; McCloskey and Nash, 1984; Dahlman, 1980; Ohlin, 1974; Parker and Jones (eds.), 1975] and hardly at all on ancient subjects [Gunderson, 1976; Cecco, 1985]. But it is not for want of data that little has been done so far. Medieval Europe had many reasons to record its activities, for taxation, and for watching dishonest subordinates. The statistics of agriculture in Europe *deteriorate* from the fourteenth to the sixteenth century.

For the classical Mediterranean the written sources are of course thin, though surprisingly rich for Roman Egypt. But the people of Mesopotamia wrote on clay; in the long run there are few limits even to quantification in such a place: get a shovel [Silver, 1983]. The statistical records of China are unsurpassed, and unexploited; those of at least British India are immense.

In any case it is not necessary to have masses of statistics to write successful historical economics. The coherence of economic theory makes it possible to leap across some of the evidential voids. The leap sounds dangerous. Any critical use of sources involves thinking, though, and economics is merely a way of thinking consistently about economies. Better to think explicitly and professionally than to fall unawares into the errors of pop economics.

The real barrier to a historical economics of earlier times or of exotic places is the breadth required in a scholar who wishes to speak on such subjects and be listened to. Alexander Gerschenkron, the great historian of European industrialisation, had more impact on economic history through his erudition and wide culture than through his findings. He embodied the mathematical penetration and scholarly expertise of the ideal historical economist. He was at the same time an economist and a historian, unifying the scientific and the humanistic halves of the culture. A scholar in training who wishes to become an historical economist of, say, Mesopotamia will want to learn French, German, Italian, Latin, Greek, Akkadian, Hebrew and Arabic, in addition to economic theory and econometrics. The prospect is daunting. Yet the opportunity to rethink histories unexamined by economics should inspire some great heart to attempt even this.

No natural limits, then, confine historical economics to the study of agriculture in the nineteenth century in America. If many of its successes so far have been won there, that is because it came to self-consciousness in places like Lafayette, Indiana, and Chicago, Illinois. Where economics can be applied – and it is the main finding of the new historical economics that it is applicable more widely than might have been supposed – there the historical economist can travel.

Notes

1. The reasoning holds only if the errors in each fragment are 'independent' of each other. If they tend to move together, then less offsetting occurs and the fall in the percentage error of the aggregate will be less. For instance, if in business depressions the reporting of statistics tended to get worse in all nine components of national income, as it well might, then errors in the various different fragments of expenditure would move together and the errors would not offset.

2. The standard deviation is only one of any number of possible ways of characterising spread. For instance, the range between highest and lowest observations, the layman's friend, is not bad for some purposes. That it is only affected by two of the observations (that is, the highest and the lowest) is a defect, corrected at slight cost by using instead the 'interquartile range', that is, the distance between the top and bottom quarters. The standard deviation, however, has an enormous and sophisticated body of thinking associated with it, an advantage that offsets its less transparent definition and calculation. It is calculated as the square root of the average of squared differences between the observations and their average. If the observations of wheat yields are five – 2.015, 4.000, 4.485, 2.500 and 2.000 – then the average is the sum (15) divided by 5, or 3.0; and the standard deviation is the square root of the average of the squared deviations from the average: $[(2.015 - 3.000)^2 + (4.000 - 3.000)^2 + (4.485 - 3.000)^2 + (2.500 - 3.000)^2 + (2.000 - 3.000)^2] / 5 = 1.085$, the square root of which is 1.04.

3. Technically, the 'least-squares' regression line is the one that makes the sum of *squares* of the divergences as small as possible. A piece of first-year calculus gives formulae for doing this with any given set of points.

4. The point is worth a little algebra, because it is left vague elsewhere in the literature, yet is not difficult; it can serve as our one example of the uses of algebra in historical economics. Suppose the price of wheat in St. Louis is P per bushel and the cost of trans-

porting the wheat from Denver to St. Louis is T per bushel (suppose that St. Louis is the place where the wheat is eaten). The Denver price, in other words, is $P - T: Denver growers get less by T because they are remote. Suppose that the *cost* of raising a bushel of wheat in Denver is C_d, and suppose the cost is in fact lower than the cost in St. Louis, C_s. Suppose the dollar amount of capital invested per bushel grown in St. Louis is K_s, and in Denver K_d. The rate of return on capital in St. Louis, then, is $(P - C_s)/K_s$, say 0.15, or 15 per cent. If there is no incentive to move capital around between the two cities (that is, if the system has settled down to rest), this return must be equal to the return in Denver, which is $(P - C_d - T)/K_d$, equal again to 15 per cent. Setting the two equal shows that the 'raw' or gross return (the return ignoring transport costs), which can be called r_d (at 15 per cent) and r_s (at something larger, because T is not reducing it: say 40 per cent), must be related this way:

$$r_d - (T/K_d) = r_s.$$

With the figures given the term T/K_d is 40 minus 15, or 25 per cent. Rearranging this last equation shows that the transport cost, T, equals the capital invested in Denver (K_d) multiplied by the advantage Denver has in 'raw' return per unit of capital (namely, 25 per cent):

$$T = (r_d - r_s) K_d.$$

So the *change* in T will equal the change of income attributable to pushing capital into Denver.

Bibliography

Abramovitz, Moses, 'Resource and Output Trends in the United States since 1870', National Bureau of Economic Research, *Occasional Paper 52* (New York, 1956).

Abramovitz, Moses and Paul David, 'Reinterpreting Economic Growth: Parables and Realities', *American Economic Review*, 62 (May 1973), 428–39.

Allen, Robert C., 'International Competition in Iron and Steel', *Journal of Economic History*, 29 (Dec. 1979), 911–37.

Allen, Robert C., 'The Efficiency and Distributional Consequences of Eighteenth-Century Enclosures', *Economic Journal*, 92 (Dec. 1982), 937–53.

Alston, Lee J., 'Farm Foreclosures in the United States During the Interwar Period', *Journal of Economic History*, 43 (Dec. 1983), 885–904.

Alston, Lee J. and Robert Higgs, 'Contractual Mix in Southern Agriculture since the Civil War: Fact, Hypotheses, and Tests', *Journal of Economic History*, 42 (June 1982), 327–54.

Ames, Edward and Nathan Rosenberg, 'The Enfield Arsenal in Theory and History', *Economic Journal*, 78 (Dec. 1968), 827–42.

Anderson, Terry, 'Wealth Estimates for the New England Colonies, 1650–1709', *Explorations in Economic History*, 12 (April 1975), 151–76.

Anderson, Terry and P. J. Hill, 'The Evolution of Property Rights: A Study of the American West', *Journal of Law and Economics*, 18 (April 1975), 163–79.

Andreano, Ralph (ed.), *The Economic Impact of the American Civil War* (Cambridge, Mass.: Schenkman, 1967).

Ankli, Robert E., 'Export-Led Growth and All That', *Explorations in Economic History*, 17 (July 1980), 251–74.

Atack, Jeremy, *Estimation of Economies of Scale in Nineteenth-Century United States Manufacturing* (New York: Garland, 1985).

Atack, Jeremy and Fred Bateman, *To Their Own Soil: American*

Agriculture in the Antebellum North (Ames, Iowa: Iowa State University Press, 1986).

Baack, Bennett D. and Edward J. Ray, 'The Political Economy of Tariff Policy: The Case of the United States', *Explorations in Economic History,* 20 (Jan. 1983), 73–93.

Baines, Dudley, 'The Labour Supply and the Labour Market 1860–1914', in Floud and McCloskey (eds), vol. 2 [1981] pp. 144–74.

Ball, Duane C. and Gary Walton, 'Agricultural Productivity Change in Eighteenth-Century Pennsylvania', *Journal of Economic History*, 36 (March 1976), 102–17.

Barnard, A., N. G. Butlin and J. J. Pincus, *Government and Capitalism: Public and Private Choice in Twentieth-Century Australia* (London: Allen and Unwin, 1982).

Bateman, Fred, 'The "Marketable Surplus" in Northern Dairy Farming: New Evidence by Size of Farm in 1860', *Agricultural History,* 52 (July 1978).

Bateman, Fred, James Foust and Thomas J. Weiss, 'Profitability in Southern Manufacturing', *Explorations in Economic History,* 12 (July 1975), 211–31.

Bean, Richard and R. P. Thomas, 'The Profits of the Slave Trade: The Fishers of Men', *Journal of Economic History,* 34 (Dec. 1974), 885–914.

Benjamin, D. J. and Levis Kochin, 'Searching for an Explanation of Unemployment in Interwar Britain', *Journal of Political Economy,* 87 (1979).

Bordo, Michael D. and Anna J. Schwartz, 'Issues in Monetary Economics and Their Impact on Research in Economic History', in R. Gallman (ed.), *Recent Developments in the Study of Business and Economic History* (Greenwich, Conn.: Johnson, 1977).

Bordo, Michael D. and Anna J. Schwartz (eds), *A Retrospective on the Classical Gold Standard, 1821–1931* (Chicago: University of Chicago Press, 1984, for the National Bureau of Economic Research).

Bos, R. W., 'Three Essays on Dutch Industrialization in the Nineteenth Century', *Afdeling Agrarische Geschiedenis, Bijdragen,* 22 (1979), 59–137, with summaries in English.

Boyer, George R., 'An Economic Model of the English Poor Law circa 1780–1834', *Explorations in Economic History,* 22 (April 1985), 129–67.

Brandt, Loren, 'Chinese Agriculture and the International

Economy, 1870–1930s: A Reassessment', *Explorations in Economic History*, 22 (April 1985), 168–93.

Brownlee, W. Elliott, *Dynamics of Ascent: A History of the American Economy* (New York: Knopf, 1974).

Brunner, K. (ed.), *The Great Depression* (Boston: Nijhoff, 1981).

Burn, Duncan, *The Economic History of Steelmaking, 1867–1939* (Cambridge: Cambridge University Press, 1961 [1940]).

Butlin, Noel, G., *Investment in Australian Economic Development 1860–1938/39* (Cambridge: Cambridge University Press, 1964).

Butlin, Noel G., *Ante-Bellum Slavery: A Critique of a Debate* (Canberra: Australian National University Press, 1971).

Butlin, Noel G., *Our Original Aggression: Aboriginal Populations of Southeastern Australia, 1788–1850* (London: Allen and Unwin, 1984).

Cain, Louis, *Sanitation Strategy for a Lakefront Metropolis: The Case of Chicago* (Dekalb, Illinois: Northern Illinois Press, 1979).

Cairncross, A. K., *Home and Foreign Investment, 1870–1913* (Cambridge: Cambridge University Press, 1953).

Capie, F. H. and M. Collins, 'The Extent of British Economic Recovery', *Economy and History*, 23 (1980).

Carlos, Ann, 'The Causes and Origins of the North American Fur Trade Rivalry, 1804–1810'. *Journal of Economic History,* 41 (Dec. 81), 777–94.

Carlson, Leonard A., 'The Dawes Act and the Decline of Indian Farming', *Journal of Economic History,* 38 (March 1978), 274–6.

Carstensen, Fred, V., *American Enterprise in Foreign Markets: Singer and International Harvester in Imperial Russia* (Chapel Hill: University of North Carolina Press, 1984).

Cecco, Marcello de, 'Monetary Theory and Roman History', *Journal of Economic History,* 45 (Dec. 1985), 809–22.

Chambers, E. J. and Gordon, Donald F., 'Primary Products and Economic Growth: An Empirical Measurement', *Journal of Political Economy,* 74 (Aug. 1966), 315–32.

Clapham, John H., 'The Study of Economic History' [1929], in N. B. Harte (ed.), *The Study of Economic History: Collected Inaugural Lectures* (London: Cass, 1971), pp. 57–70.

Clapham, John H., 'Economic History as a Discipline'. Reprinted from the *Encyclopedia of the Social Sciences* [1930] in F. C. Lane and J. C.Riemersma (eds), *Enterprise and Secular Change* (Homewood, Illinois: Irwin, 1953).

Coatsworth, John, *Growth Against Development: The Economic Impact of Railroads in Porfirian Mexico* (De Kalb, Illinois: University of Northern Illinois Press, 1981).

Coelho, Philip R. P., 'The Profitability of Imperialism: The British Experience in the West Indies, 1768–1772', *Explorations in Economic History*, 10 (Spring 1973), 253–80.

Cohen, Jon S., 'Fascism and Agriculture in Italy: Policies and Consequences', *Economic History Review*, 32 (Feb. 1979), 70–87.

Cooley, T. F. and Stephen J. DeCanio, 'Rational Expectations in American Agriculture, 1867–1914', *Review of Economics and Statistics*, 59 (Feb. 1977), 9–17.

Conference on Research in Income and Wealth, *Trends in the American Economy in the Nineteenth Century*. Studies in Income and Wealth, vol. 24 (Princeton: Princeton University Press, 1960).

Conference on Research in Income and Wealth, *Output, Employment, and Productivity in the United States after 1800*. Studies in Income and Wealth, vol. 30 (New York: Columbia University Press, 1966).

Conrad, Alfred and John R. Meyer, 'The Economics of Slavery in the Ante Bellum South', *Journal of Political Economy*, 66 (Oct. 1958), 442–43.

Coulton, G. G., *The Medieval Village* (Cambridge: Cambridge University Press, 1931).

Crafts, N. F. R., 'Gross National Product in Europe 1870–1910: Some New Estimates', *Explorations in Economic History*, 20 (Oct. 1983), 387–401.

Crafts, N. F. R., *British Economic Growth during the Industrial Revolution* (New York and London: Oxford University Press, 1985).

Dahlman, Carl. J., *The Open Field System and Beyond* (Cambridge: Cambridge University Press, 1980).

David, Paul A., 'The Growth of Real Product in the United States Before 1840: New Evidence, Controlled Conjectures', *Journal of Economic History*, 27 (June 1967), 151–97.

David, Paul A., 'Transport Innovation and Economic Growth: Professor Fogel on and Off the Rails', *Economic History Review*, 22 (Dec. 1969), 506–25; reprinted in David [1975].

David, Paul A., 'The Landscape and the Machine: Technical Interrelatedness, Land Tenure and the Mechanization of the Corn Harvest in Victorian Britain', in D. N. McCloskey (ed.), *Essays on a Mature Economy: Britain after 1840* (London: Methuen, 1971) pp. 145–205; reprinted in David (ed.) [1975].

David, Paul A, *Technical Choice, Innovation and Economic Growth: Essays on American and British Experience in the Nineteenth Century* (Cambridge: Cambridge University Press, 1975).

David, Paul A., Herbert Gutman, Richard Sutch, Peter Temin and Gavin Wright, *Reckoning with Slavery: A Critical Study of the Quantitative History of American Negro Slavery* (Oxford: Oxford University Press, 1972).

Davis, Lance E., 'The Investment Market, 1870–1914: The Evolution of a National Market', *Journal of Economic History*, 25 (Sept. 1965), 355–99; reprinted in *Purdue Faculty Papers* [1967].

Davis, Lance E. and Douglass North, with the assistance of Calla Smorodin, *Institutional Change and American Economic Growth* (Cambridge: Cambridge University Press, 1971).

Davis, Lance E., Richard A. Easterlin, William N. Parker *et al.*, *American Economic Growth: An Economist's History of the United States* (New York: Harper and Row, 1972).

Davis, Lance E. and Robert Huttenback, 'The Political Economy of British Imperialism: Measures of Benefit and Support', *Journal of Economic History*, 42 (Mar. 1982), 119–30.

Deane, Phyllis and W. A. Cole, *British Economic Growth, 1688–1959*, 2nd edn (Cambridge: Cambridge University Press, 1967).

DeCanio, Stephen, *Agriculture in the Postbellum South: The Economics of Production and Supply* (Cambridge: M. I. T. Press, 1974).

De Meere, J. M. M., 'Growth and Inequality in Amsterdam, 1877–1940', *Tijdschrift Voor Sociale Geschiedenis*, 13 (1979), 3–47.

Denison, Edward, *The Sources of Economic Growth in the United States* (New York: Committee for Economic Development, 1962).

Dick, Trevor J. O., 'United States Railroad Inventions': Investment since 1870', *Explorations in Economic History*, 11 (Spring 1974), 249–70.

Dick, Trevor J. O., *Economic History of Canada: A Guide to Information Sources* (Detroit: Gale, 1977).

Dick, Trevor J. O., 'Canadian Wheat Production and Trade, 1896–1930', *Explorations in Economic History*, 17 (July 1980), 275–302.

Dumke, Rolf H., 'Intra-German Trade in 1837 and Regional Economic Development', *Vierteljahrschrift für Sozial – und Wirtschaftsgeschichte*, 64 (1977), 468–96.

Dunlevy, J. A. and H. A. Gemery, 'British-Irish Settlement Patterns in the United States: The Role of Family and Friends', *Scottish*

Journal of Political Economy, 24 (Nov. 1977), 257–63.

Easterlin, Richard A., 'Regional Income Trends, 1840–1950', in S. Harris (ed.), *American Economic History* (New York: McGraw-Hill, 1961), pp. 525–47, reprinted in Fogel and Engerman (eds) [1971].

Easterlin, Richard A., *Population, Labor Force, and Long Swings in American Economic Growth* (New York: National Bureau of Economic Research, 1968).

Easton, Stephen T., 'The Outdoor Relief System in England and Wales', in H. G. Grubel and M. A. Walker (eds), *Unemployment Insurance: Global Evidence of Its Effects on Unemployment* (Vancouver: Fraser Institute, 1978), pp. 320–38.

Eddie, Scott, M., 'The Terms and Patterns of Hungarian Foreign Trade, 1882–1913', *Journal of Economic History*, 37 (June 1977), 329–58.

Edelstein, Michael, 'Realized Rates of Return on U.K. Home and Overseas Investment in the Age of High Imperialism', *Explorations in Economic History*, 13 (July 1976), 283–329.

Edelstein, Michael, *Overseas Investment in the Age of High Imperialism* (New York: Columbia University Press, 1982).

Eichengreen, Barry, 'Did Speculation Destabilize the French Franc in the 1920s?' *Explorations in Economic History*, 19 (Jan. 1982), 71–100.

Eichengreen, Barry (ed.), *Sterling and the Tariff* (Princeton: Princeton University Press, for the International Finance Section, Department of Economics, 1981).

Eichengreen, Barry (ed.), *The Gold Standard in Theory and History* (London and New York: Methuen, 1985).

Eichengreen, Barry and Jeffrey Sachs, 'Exchange Rates and Economic Recovery in the 1930s', *Journal of Economic History*, 45 (Dec. 1985), 925–46.

Elbaum, Bernard and William Lazonick, 'The Decline of the British Economy: An Institutional Perspective', *Journal of Economic History*, 44 (June 1984), 467–84.

Elster, Jon, *Logic and Society: Contradictions and Possible Worlds* (Chichester and New York: Wiley, 1978).

Engerman, Stanley, 'The Economic Impact of the Civil War', *Explorations in Economic History*, 3 (Spring/Summer 1966), 176–99.

Engerman, Stanley, 'Some Considerations Relating to Property Rights in Man', *Journal of Economic History*, 33 (Mar. 1973), 43–65.

Engerman, Stanley, 'Economic Change and Contract Labor in the British Carribean: The End of Slavery and the Adjustment to Emancipation', *Explorations in Economic History,* 21 (Apr. 1984), 133–51.

Engerman, Stanley and H. S. Klein, 'A Note on the Mortality in the French Slave Trade in the Eighteenth Century', in Gemery and Hogendorn (eds) [1979].

Enthoven, Alain, C., 'Economic Analysis in the Department of Defense', *American Economic Review,* 53 (May 1963), 413–23.

Feeny, David H., 'Paddy, Princes, and Productivity: Irrigation and Thai Agricultural Development, 1900–1940', *Explorations in Economic History,* 16 (Apr. 1979), 132–50.

Feinstein, Charles H., *National Income, Expenditure and Output of the United Kingdom 1855–1965* (Cambridge University Press, 1972).

Feinstein, Charles H., 'Capital Formation in Great Britain', in P. Mathias and M. M. Postan (eds), *The Cambridge Economic History of Europe,* vol. VII, part I (Cambridge University Press, 1978), pp. 28–96.

Felix, David, 'De Gustibus Disputandum Est: Changing Consumer Preferences in Economic Growth', *Explorations in Economic History,* 16 (July 1979), 260–96.

Fenoaltea, Stefano, 'Public Policy and Italian Industrial Development, 1861–1913', *Journal of Economic History,* 29 (Mar. 1969), 176–9.

Fenoaltea, Stefano, 'Slavery and Supervision in Comparative Perspective: A Model', *Journal of Economic History,* 44 (Sept. 1984), 635–68.

Fenoaltea, Stefano, *Italian Industrial Production, 1861–1914: A Statistical Reconstruction* (Cambridge University Press, forthcoming).

Field, Alexander, 'Sectoral Shift in Antebellum Massachusetts: A Reconsideration', *Explorations in Economic History,* 15 (Apr. 1978), 146–71.

Field, Alexander, 'Land Abundance, Interest/Profit Rates, and Nineteenth-Century American and British Technology', *Journal of Economic History,* 43 (June 1983), 405–32.

Fishlow, Albert, *American Railroads and the Transformation of the Antebellum Economy* (Cambridge: Harvard University Press, 1965).

Fishlow, Albert, 'Productivity and Technological Change in the Railroad Sector, 1840–1910', in Conference on Income, vol. 30 [1966], pp. 583–646.

Floud, Roderick (ed.), *Essays in Quantitative Economic History* (Oxford: Oxford University Press, 1974).

Floud, Roderick, *The British Machine Tool Industry 1850–1914* (Cambridge University Press, 1976).

Floud, Roderick, *An Introduction to Quantitative Methods for Historians,* 2nd edn (London: Methuen, 1979).

Floud, Roderick, and D. N. McCloskey (eds), *The Economic History of Britain since 1700,* vol. 1: 1700–1860; vol. 2: 1860 to the 1970s (Cambridge University Press, 1981).

Flynn, Dennis O., 'A New Perspective on the Spanish Price Revolution: The Monetary Approach to the Balance of Payments', *Explorations in Economic History,* 15 (Oct. 1978), 388–406.

Fogel, Robert, W., *Railroads and American Economic Growth: Essays in Econometric History* (Baltimore: John Hopkins University Press, 1964).

Fogel, Robert W., 'The Specification Problem in Economic History', *Journal of Economic History,* 27 (Sept. 1967), 283–308.

Fogel, Robert W., 'Notes on the Social Saving Controversy', *Journal of Economic History,* 39 (Mar. 1979), 1–54.

Fogel, Robert W. and Stanley L. Engerman, 'A Model for the Explanation of Industrial Expansion During the Nineteenth Century: With an Application to the American Iron Industry', *Journal of Political Economy,* 77 (May/June 1969), 306–28; reprinted in Fogel and Engerman (eds) [1971].

Fogel, Robert W. and Stanley L. Engerman (eds), *The Reinterpretation of American Economic History* (New York: Harper and Row, 1971).

Fogel, Robert W. and Stanley L. Engerman, *Time on the Cross: The Economics of American Negro Slavery* (Boston: Little, Brown, 1974).

Ford, A. G., *The Gold Standard, 1880–1914: Britain and Argentina* (Oxford: Oxford University Press, 1962).

Foreman-Peck, James, 'Tariff Protection and Economies of Scale: The British Motor Industry Before 1939', *Oxford Economic Papers,* 31 (July 1979), 237–57.

Forster, Colin (ed.), *Australian Economic Development in the Twentieth Century* (London: George Allen & Unwin, 1970).

Frankel, Marvin, 'Obsolescence and Technological Change in a Maturing Economy', *American Economic Review,* 45 (June 1955), 296–319.

Fremdling, Rainer, 'Railroads and German Economic Growth: A Leading Sector Analysis with a Comparison to the United States and Great Britain', *Journal of Economic History*, 37 (Sept. 1977), 419–43.

Freudenberger, Herman and J. G. Cummins, 'Health, Work, and Leisure before the Industrial Revolution', *Explorations in Economic History*, 13 (Jan. 1976), 1–12.

Friedman, Milton and Anna J. Schwartz, *A Monetary History of the United States, 1867–1960* (Princeton: Princeton University Press, 1963).

Friedman, Milton and Anna J. Schwartz, *Monetary Trends in the United States and the United Kingdom, 1867–1975* (Chicago: University of Chicago Press, 1982).

Friedman, Philip, 'An Econometric Model of National Income, Commercial Policy and the Level of International Trade: The Open Economies of Europe, 1924–1938', *Journal of Economic History, 38* (Mar. 1978), 148–80.

Galenson, David, *White Servitude in Colonial America: An Economic Analysis* (Cambridge University Press, 1981).

Galenson, David, *Traders, Planters and Slaves: Market Behavior in Early English America* (Cambridge University Press, 1986).

Gallaway, Lowell and Richard K. Vedder, 'Emigration from the United Kingdom to the United States: 1860–1913', *Journal of Economic History*, 31 (Dec. 1971), 885–97.

Gallman, Robert, 'Gross National Product in the United States, 1834–1909', in Conference on Income [1966], pp. 3–76.

Gallman, Robert and Edward S. Howle, 'Trends in the Structure of the American Economy since 1840', in Fogel and Engerman (eds). [1971], pp. 25–37.

Gayer, A. D., W. W. Rostow and Anna J. Schwartz, *The Growth and Fluctuation of the British Economy, 1790–1850: An Historical, Statistical and Theoretical Study* (Oxford: Oxford University Press, 1953).

Gemery, Henry A., 'Emigration from the British Isles to the New World, 1630–1700: Inferences from Colonial Populations', *Research in Economic History*, 5 (1980) 179–231.

Gemery, Henry A. and Jan S. Hogendorn, 'The Atlantic Slave Trade: A Tentative Economic Model', *Journal of African History*, 15 (1974), 223–46.

Gemery, Henry A. and Jan S. Hogendorn (eds), *The Uncommon*

Market: Essays in the Economic History of the Atlantic Slave Trade (New York: Academic Press, 1979).

George, Peter and E. H. Oksanen, 'An Index of Aggregate Economic Activity in Canada, 1896–1939: A Factor Analytic Approach', *Explorations in Economic History*, 17 (Apr. 1980), 118–34.

Gerschenkron, Alexander, 'Description of an Index of Italian Industrial Development, 1881–1913', in his *Economic Backwardness in Historical Perspective* (Cambridge: Harvard University Press, 1962), pp. 367–421.

Goldin, Claudia, D., *Urban Slavery in the American South, 1820–1860* (Chicago: University of Chicago Press, 1976).

Goldin, Claudia D., 'The Historical Evolution of Female Earnings, Functions and Occupations', *Explorations in Economic History*, 21 (Jan. 1984), 1–27.

Goldin, Claudia D. and Frank Lewis, 'The Economic Cost of the American Civil War: Estimates and Implications', *Journal of Economic History*, 35 (June 1975), 299–326.

Goldsmith, Raymond *et al.*, *A Study of Savings in the United States* (Princeton: Princeton University Press, 1965).

Good, David F., *The Economic Rise of the Habsburg Empire, 1750–1914* (Berkeley: University of California Press, 1984).

Gould, John D., *The Great Debasement of the Economy in Mid-Tudor England* (Oxford: Oxford University Press, 1970).

Grantham, George, 'Scale and Organization in French Farming, 1840–1880', in Parker and Jones (eds) [1975], pp. 293–326.

Grantham, George, 'The Persistence of Open Field Farming in Nineteenth-Century France', *Journal of Economic History*, 40 (Sept. 1980), 515–31.

Graves, Robert and Alan Hodge, *The Reader Over Your Shoulder* (New York: Macmillan, 1961) [1943].

Gray, Ralph and John M. Peterson, *Economic Development of the United States*, rev. edn. (Homewood, Illinois: Irwin, 1974).

Gregory, Paul, 'Some Empirical Comments on the Theory of Relative Backwardness: The Russian Case', *Economic Development and Cultural Change*, 22 (July 1974), 654–65.

Gregory, Paul, *Russian National Income, 1855–1913*. (Cambridge: Cambridge University Press, 1984).

Gunderson, Gerald, 'Economic Change and the Demise of the

Roman Empire', *Explorations in Economic History*, 13 (Jan. 1976), 43–68.

Haig, Bryan D. and Neville G. Cain, 'Industrialization and Productivity: Australian Manufacturing in the 1920s and 1930s', *Explorations in Economic History*, 20 (Apr. 1983), 183–98.

Haines, Michael, *Fertility and Occupation: Population Pattern in Industrialization* (New York: Academic Press, 1979).

Hamilton, Earl J., *American Treasure and the Price Revolution in Spain, 1501–1650* (Cambridge: Harvard University Press, 1934).

Hamilton, Earl J., *Money, Prices and Wages in Valencia, Aragon and Navarre, 1351–1500* (Cambridge: Harvard University Press, 1936).

Hamilton, Earl J., *War and Prices in Spain, 1651–1800* (Cambridge: Harvard University Press, 1947).

Hannah, Leslie and J. A. Kay, *Concentration in Modern Industry: Theory, Measurement and the U.K. Experience* (London: Macmillan, 1977).

Hannon, Joan Underhill, 'Ethnic Discrimination in a 19th-Century Mining District: Michigan Copper Mines, 1888', *Explorations in Economic History*, 19 (Jan. 1982), 28–50.

Harley, C. K., 'The Shift from Sailing Ships to Steam Ships, 1850–1890', in McCloskey (ed.) [1971], pp. 215–31.

Harley, C. K., 'Skilled Labour and the Choice of Technique in Edwardian Industry', *Explorations in Economic History*, 11 (Summer 1974), 391–414.

Harley, C. K., 'British Industrialization Before 1841: Evidence of Slower Growth During the Industrial Revolution', *Journal of Economic History*, 42 (June 1982), 267–90.

Hartwell, R. M. and Stanley L. Engerman, 'Models of Immiseration: The Theoretical Basis of Pessimism', in A. J. Taylor (ed.), *The Standard of Living in Britain in the Industrial Revolution* (London: Methuen, 1975), pp. 189–213.

Hausman, William J., 'Cheap Coal or Limitation of the Vend: The London Coal Trade, 1770–1845', *Journal of Economic History*, 44 (June 1984), 345–54.

Hawke, Gary, *Railways and Economic Growth in England and Wales, 1840–1870* (Oxford: Oxford University Press, 1970).

Hawke, Gary, *Economics for Historians* (Cambridge: Cambridge University Press 1980).

Heckscher, Eli, F., 'Natural and Money Economy, as Illustrated from Swedish History in the Sixteenth Century', *Journal of Economic and Business History*, 3 (Nov. 1930), 1–29.

Henning, Graydon R. and Keith Trace, 'Britain and the Motorship: A Case of the Delayed Adoption of New Technology?' *Journal of Economic History*, 35 (June 1975), 353–85.

Heston, Alan and Dharma Kumar, 'The Persistence of Land Fragmentation in Peasant Agriculture: An Analysis of South Asian Cases', *Explorations in Economic History*, 20 (Apr. 1983), 199–220.

Higgs, Robert, 'Race, Skills, and Earnings: American Immigrants in 1900', *Journal of Political Economy*, 79 (May–June 1971)a, 661–7.

Higgs, Robert, *The Transformation of the American Economy, 1865–1914: An Essay in Interpretation* (New York: Wiley, 1971)b.

Higgs, Robert, *Competition and Coercion: Blacks in the American Economy, 1865–1914* (Cambridge: Cambridge University Press 1977).

Higgs, Robert, *Crisis and Leviathan: Critical Episodes in the Emergence of the Mixed Economy* (Cambridge, Mass.: Ballinger, 1987).

Hoffmann, Walther, G., *British Industry 1700–1950*, trans. W. O. Henderson and W. H. Chaloner (Oxford: Oxford University Press, 1955) [1939].

Hoffmann, Walther, G., *Das Wachstum der deutschen Wirtschaft seit der Mitte des 19. Jahrhunderts* (Berlin: Springer, 1965).

Hogendorn, Jan S., *Nigerian Groundnut Exports: Origins and Early Development* (London and Zaria: Oxford University Press and Ahmadu Bello University Press, 1979).

Hohenberg, Paul, 'Change in Rural France in the Period of Industrialization, 1830–1914', *Journal of Economic History*, 32 (Mar. 1972), 219–40.

Hohenberg, Paul and Lynn H. Lees, *The Making of Urban Europe, 1000–1950* (Cambridge: Cambridge University Press 1985).

Howson, Susan, *Domestic Monetary Management in Britain, 1919–38* (Cambridge: Cambridge University Press, 1975).

Hueckel, Glenn, 'War and the British Economy, 1793–1815: A General Equilibrium Analysis', *Explorations in Economic History*, 10 (Summer 1973), 265–96.

Hughes, J. R. T., *Fluctuations in Trade, Industry and Finance: A Study of British Economic Development 1850–60* (Oxford: Oxford University Press, 1960).

Hughes, J. R. T., *The Governmental Habit* (New York: Basic Books, 1977).

Hughes, J. R.T., *Social Control in the Colonial Economy* (Charlottesville: University of Virginia Press, 1981).

Hughes, J. R. T., *American Economic History* (Glenview, Illinois: Scott, Foresman, 1983).

Hughes, J. R. T. and Stanley Reiter, 'The First 1,945 British Steamships', *Journal of the American Statistical Association,* 53 (June 1958), 360–81; reprinted in *Purdue Faculty Papers* [1967].

Hutchinson, William K., *American Economic History: A Guide to Information Sources* (Detroit: Gale, 1980).

Hyde, Charles K., *Technological Change in the British Iron Industry 1700–1870* (Princeton: Princeton University Press, 1977).

Imlah, Albert H., *Economic Elements in the Pax Britannica* (Cambridge: Harvard University Press, 1958).

Ippolito, Richard A., 'The Effect of the Agricultural Depression on Industrial Demand in England: 1730–1750', *Economica*, 42 (Aug. 1975), 298–312.

James, John A., *Money and Capital Markets in Postbellum America* (Princeton: Princeton University Press, 1978).

James, John A., 'The Welfare Effects of the Antebellum Tariff: A General Equilibrium Analysis', *Explorations in Economic History*, 15 (July 1978), 231–56.

James, John A., 'The Use of General Equilibrium Analysis in Economic History', *Explorations in Economic History,* 21 (July 1984), 231–53.

Jones, Alice H., *The Wealth of a Nation to Be: The American Colonies on the Eve of the Revolution* (New York: Columbia University Press, 1980).

Jones, S. R. H., 'Price Associations and Competition in the British Pin Industry, 1814–40', *Economic History Review, 26 (May 1973),* 237–52.

Jonung, Lars, 'Monetization and the Behavior of Velocity in Sweden, 1871–1913', *Explorations in Economic History,* 20 (Oct. 1983), 418–39.

Jorberg, Lennart and T. Bengtsson, 'Market Integration in Sweden during the 18th and 19th Centuries: Spectral Analysis of Grain Prices', *Economy and History,* 18 (1975).

Kearl, J. R., Clayne Pope and L. T. Wimmer, 'Household Wealth in a Settlement Economy: Utah, 1850–70', *Journal of Economic*

History, 40 (Sept. 1980), 477–96.

Kelley, Allen C. and J. G. Williamson, *Lessons from Japanese Development: An Analytic Economic History* (Chicago: University of Chicago Press, 1974).

Kennedy, William P., 'Foreign Investment, Trade and Growth in the United Kingdom, 1870–1913', *Explorations in Economic History,* 11 (Summer 1974), 415–44.

Kessel, R. A. and Armen Alchian, 'Real Wages in the North During the Civil War: Mitchell's Data Reinterpreted', *Journal of Law and Economics,* 2 (Oct. 1959), 95–113; reprinted in Fogel and Engerman (eds) [1971].

Kindleberger, C. P., *The Terms of Trade: A European Case Study* (Cambridge: M.I.T. Press, 1956).

Kindleberger, C. P., *Economic Growth in France and Britain 1851–1950* (Cambridge: Harvard University Press, 1964).

Kindleberger, C. P., *The World in Depression 1929–1939* (Berkeley and Los Angeles: University of California Press, 1973).

Klingaman, David, Richard Vedder and Lowell Gallaway, 'Discrimination and Exploitation in Antebellum Cotton Textile Manufacturing', *Research in Economic History,* 3 (1978), 217–62.

Komlos, John, *The Habsburg Monarchy as a Customs Union: Economic Development in Austria-Hungary in the Nineteenth Century* (Princeton: Princeton University Press, 1983)a.

Komlos, John (ed.), *Economic Development in the Habsburg Monarchy in the Nineteenth Century: Essays. Eastern European Quarterly,* East European Monographs, (1983)b.

Kumar, Dharma and Meghnad Desai (eds), *The Cambridge Economic History of India,* vol. 2 (Cambridge: Cambridge University Press, 1983).

Kuznets, Simon, *European Economic Growth: Rate, Structure and Spread* (New Haven: Yale University Press, 1966).

Latham, A. J. H., 'Merchandise Trade Imbalances and Uneven Economic Development in India and China', *Journal of European Economic History,* 7 (1978), 33–60.

Lazonick, William, 'Factor Costs and the Diffusion of Ring Spinning in Britain Prior to World War 1', *Quarterly Journal of Economics,* 96 (1981), 89–109.

Lazonick, William, 'Production Relations, Labor Productivity, and Choice of Technique: British and U.S. Cotton Spinning', *Journal of Economic History,* 41 (Sept. 1981), 491–516.

Lazonick, William and Thomas Brush, 'The "Horndal Effect" in Early U. S. Manufacturing', *Explorations in Economic History*, 22 (Jan. 1985), 53–96.

Lebergott, Stanley, *Manpower in Economic Growth: The American Record since 1800* (New York: W. W. Norton, 1964).

Lebergott, Stanley, *The American Economy: Income, Wealth and Want* (Princeton: Princeton University Press, 1976).

Lebergott, Stanley, 'The Returns to U.S. Imperialism, 1890–1929', *Journal of Economic History*, 40 (June 1980), 229–52.

Lebergott, Stanley, *The Americans: An Economic Record* (New York: Norton, 1984).

Lee, C. H., *Regional Economic Growth in the United Kingdom since the 1880s* (London: McGraw-Hill, 1971).

Lee, C. H., *Social Science and History: An Investigation into the Application of Theory and Quantification in British Economic and Social History* (London: Social Science Research Council, 1983).

Lee, Ronald Demos (ed.), *Population Patterns in the Past* (New York: Academic Press, 1977).

Lee, Susan Previant and Pater Passell, *A New Economic View of American Economic History* (New York: Norton, 1979).

Leff, Nathaniel, *The Brazilian Capital-Goods Industry, 1929–1964* (Cambridge: Harvard University Press, 1968).

Leff, Nathaniel, *Economic Retardation and Economic Progress in Brazil, 1822–1947* (forthcoming).

Lewis, Frank and Marvin McInnis, 'The Efficiency of the French-Canadian Farmer in the Nineteenth Century', *Journal of Economic History*, 40 (Sept. 1980), 497–514.

Lewis, W. Arthur, *Tropical Development, 1883–1913* (London: Allen and Unwin, 1970).

Lewis, W. Arthur, *Growth and Fluctuations, 1870–1913* (London: Allen and Unwin, 1978).

Libecap, Gary D., 'Economic Variables and the Development of the Law: The Case of Western Mineral Rights', *Journal of Economic History*, 38 (June 1978), 338–62.

Libecap, Gary D., 'The Political Allocation of Mineral Rights: A Re-evaluation of Teapot Dome', *Journal of Economic History*, 44 (June 1984), 381–92.

Lindert, Peter H., *Fertility and Scarcity in America* (Princeton: Princeton University Press, 1978).

Lindert, Peter H., 'English Occupations, 1670–1811', *Journal of*

Economic History, 40 (Dec. 1980), 685–712.

Lindert, Peter H. and Keith Trace, 'Yardsticks for Victorian Enterpreneurs', in McCloskey, (ed.) [1971], pp. 239–74.

Lyons, John S., 'The Lancashire Cotton Industry and the Introduction of the Power Loom, 1815–1850', Ph.D. dissertation, University of California, Berkeley, 1977.

MacColl, Ewan, *The Shuttle and the Cage: Industrial Folk Ballads* (New York: Hargail, 1954).

MacKinnon, Mary, 'Poverty and Policy: The English Poor Law, 1860–1914', *Journal of Economic History,* 46 (June 1986).

Mak, James, Eric Haites and Gary Walton, *Western River Transportation: The Era of Early Internal Development, 1810–1860* (Baltimore: Johns Hopkins University Press, 1975).

Marglin, Stephen, 'What Do Bosses Do?' in A. Gorz (ed.), *The Division of Labour* (London: Longmans, 1976), pp. 13–54.

Margo, Robert A., 'Teacher Salaries in Black and White', *Explorations in Economic History,* 21 (July 1984), 306–27.

Marr, W. L. and D. G. Patterson, *Canada: An Economic History* (Toronto: Macmillan of Canada, 1980).

Matthews, R. C. O., *A Study in Trade Cycle History: Economic Fluctuations in Great Britain, 1833–42* (Cambridge: Cambridge University Press, 1954).

Matthews, R. C. O., Charles H. Feinstein and J. C. Odling-Smee, *British Economic Growth 1856–1973* (Oxford: Oxford University Press, 1982).

McAlpin, Michelle, 'Price Movements and Fluctuations in Economic Activity, 1860–1947', in Kumar and Desai (eds) [1983]a.

McAlpin, Michelle, *Subject to Famine: Food Crisis and Economic Change in Western India 1860–1920* (Princeton: Princeton University Press, 1983)b.

McClelland, Peter D., 'The Cost to America of British Imperial Policy', *American Economic Review,* 59 (May 1969), 370–81.

McClelland, Peter D., *Casual Explanation and Model Building in History, Economics, and the New Economic History* (Ithaca: Cornell University Press, 1975).

McClelland, Peter D., 'Transportation', in G. Porter (ed.) [1980], pp. 309–34.

McCloskey, D. N., 'Did Victorian Britain Fail?' *Economic History Review,* 23 (Dec. 1970), 446–459; reprinted in McCloskey [1981].

McCloskey, D.N. (ed.), *Essays on a Mature Economy: Britain after 1840 (London: Methuen, 1971)*.

McCloskey, D. N., *Economic Maturity and Entrepreneurial Decline: British Iron and Steel, 1870–1913* (Cambridge: Harvard University Press, 1973).

McCloskey, D. N., 'The Economics of Enclosure: A Market Analysis', in Parker and Jones, (eds) [1975], pp. 123–60.

McCloskey, D. N., 'English Open Fields as Behavior Towards Risk', *Research in Economic History*, 1 (Fall 1976), 124–70.

McCloskey, D. N. *Enterprise and Trade in Victorian Britain: Essays in Historical Economics* (London: Allen and Unwin, 1981).

McCloskey, D. N. and George Hersh, Jr, *A Bibliography of Historical Economics 1958–1980* (Cambridge: Cambridge University Press 1988).

McCloskey, D. N. and John Nash, 'Corn at Interest: The Cost and Extent of Grain Storage in Medieval England', *American Economic Review*, 74 (Mar. 1984), 174–87.

McGouldrick, Paul F., *New England Textiles in the Nineteenth Century: Profits and Investment* (Cambridge: Harvard University Press 1968).

McGouldrick, Paul F. and Michael B. Tannen, 'Did American Manufacturers Discriminate Against Immigrants before 1914?' *Journal of Economic History*, 37 (Sept. 1977), 723–46.

McHugh, Cathy L., 'Earnings in the Post-bellum Southern Cotton Textile Industry: A Case Study', *Explorations in Economic History*, 21 (Jan. 1984), 28–39.

McInnis, Marvin, 'Childbearing and Land Availability: Some Evidence from Individual Household data,' in Lee (ed) [1977], pp. 201–27.

McLean, Ian W., 'The Adoption of Harvest Machinery in Victoria in the Late Nineteenth Century', *Australian Economic History Review*, 13 (Mar. 1973), 41–56.

Meeker, Edward, 'The Social Rate of Return on Investment in Public Health, 1880–1911', *Journal of Economic History*, 34 (June 1974), 392–421.

Mendels, Franklin, 'Protoindustrialization: The First Phase of the Industrialization Process', *Journal of Economic History*, 32 (Mar. 1972), 241–61.

Mercer, Lloyd J. and W. Douglas Morgan, 'Alternative Interpretations of Market Saturation: Evaluation for the Automobile

Market in the Late Twenties', *Explorations in Economic History*, 9 (Spring 1972), 269–90.

Metzer, Jacob, 'Railroad Development and Market Integration: The Case of Tsarist Russia', *Journal of Economic History*, 34 (Sept. 1974), 529–50.

Metzer, Jacob and Oded Kaplan, 'Jointly But Severally: Arab-Jewish Dualism in Mandatory Palestine', *Journal of Economic History*, 45 (June 1985), 327–45.

Mirowski, Philip, 'The Rise (and Retreat) of a Market: English Joint Stocks in the Eighteenth Century', *Journal of Economic History*, 41 (Sept. 1981), 559–77.

Mitch, David, 'Underinvestment in Literacy? The Potential Contribution of Government Involvement in Elementary Education to Economic Growth in Nineteenth-Century England', *Journal of Economic History*, 44 (June 1984), 557–66.

Mitchell, B. R., with the assistance of Phyllis Deane, *Abstract of British Historical Statistics* (Cambridge: Cambridge University Press 1962).

Moggridge, Donald, *British Monetary Policy, 1924–1931: The Norman Conquest of $4.86* (Cambridge: Cambridge University Press 1962).

Mokyr, Joel, *Industrialization in the Low Countries, 1795–1850* (New Haven: Yale University Press, 1976).

Mokyr, Joel, 'Demand vs. Supply in the Industrial Revolution', *Journal of Economic History*, 37 (Dec. 1977), 981–1008.

Mokyr, Joel, *Why Ireland Starved* (London: Allen and Unwin, 1983).

Mokyr, Joel (ed.), *The Economics of the Industrial Revolution* (Totowa, N. J.: Rowman and Allanheld, 1985).

Mokyr, Joel and N. Eugene Savin, 'Stagflation in Historical Perspective: The Napoleonic Wars Revisited', *Research in Economic History*, 1 (1976), 198–259.

Morgenstern, Oskar, *On the Accuracy of Economic Observations*, 2nd edn (Princeton: Princeton University Press 1963).

Morris, Cynthia Taft and Irma Adelman, 'Patterns of Industrialization in the Nineteenth and Early Twentieth Centuries: A Cross-Sectional Quantitative Study', *Research in Economic History*, 5 (1980), 1–83.

Morris, M. D., *The Emergence of an Industrial Labor Force in Bombay: A Study of the Bombay Cotton Mills 1854–1947* (Berkeley: University of California Press, 1965).

Morris, M. D., 'Industrialisation in South Asia, 1800–1947', in Kumar and Desai (eds.) [1983].

Mosk, Carl. A., 'Fecundity, Infanticide and Food Consumption in Japan', *Explorations in Economic History,* 15 (July 1978), 269–89.

Munyon, Paul, 'A Critical Review of Estimates of Net Income from Agriculture from 1880 and 1900: New Hampshire, a Case Study', *Journal of Economic History,* 37 (Sept. 1977), 634–54.

Nardinelli, Clark, 'Child Labor and the Factory Acts', *Journal of Economic History,* 40 (Dec. 1980), 739–55.

Neal, Larry D., 'Investment Behavior by American Railroads: 1897–1914', *Review of Economics and Statistics,* 51 (May 1969), 126–35.

Neal, Larry D., 'Cross Spectral Analysis of Atlantic Migration', *Research in Economic History,* 1 (1976), 260–97.

Neal, Larry D. and Paul Uselding, 'Immigration: A Neglected Source of American Economic Growth, 1790 to 1912', *Oxford Economic Papers,* 24 (Mar. 1972), 68–88.

Neuberger, Hugh and H. H. Stokes, 'German Banks and German Growth, 1883–1913', *Journal of Economic History,* 34 (Sept. 1974), 710–31.

Neuhaus, Paulo (ed.), *A Economia Brasileira: uma Visao Historica* (Rio de Janeiro: Editora Campus, 1979).

Newell, William, 'The Agricultural Revolution in Nineteenth-Century France', *Journal of Economic History,* 33 (Dec. 1973), 697–731.

Nicholas, Stephen, 'Agency Contracts, Institutional Modes, and the Transition to Foreign Direct Investment by British Manufacturing Multinationals Before 1939', *Journal of Economic History,* 43 (Sept. 1983), 675–86.

Nickless, Pamela, 'A New Look at Productivity in New England Cotton Textiles, 1836–1860', *Journal of Economic History 39,* (Dec. 1979), 889–910.

Niemi, Albert W., Jr, *State and Regional Patterns in American Manufacturing, 1860–1900* (Westport, Conn.: Greenwood Press, 1974).

Niemi, Albert W., Jr, *U.S. Economic History: A Survey of the Major Issues* (Chicago: Rand McNally, 1975).

North, Douglass C., 'Sources of Productivity Change in Ocean Shipping, 1600–1850', *Journal of Political Economy,* 76 (Sept/Oct 1968), 953–70; reprinted in Fogel and Engerman (eds) [1971].

North, Douglass C., 'Government and the Cost of Exchange in

History', *Journal of Economic History,* 44 (June 1984), 255–64.

North, Douglass C., Terry L. Anderson and Peter J. Hill, *Growth and Welfare in the American Past: A New Economic History,* 3rd edn (Englewood Cliffs, N.J.: Prentice-Hall, 1983).

North, Douglass, C. and Robert Paul Thomas, *The Rise of the Western World: A New Economic History* (Cambridge: Cambridge University Press 1973).

O'Brien, Patrick, *The New Economic History of the Railways* (New York: St. Martin's Press, 1977).

O'Brien, Patrick and Stanley Engerman, 'Changes in Income and Its Distribution During the Industrial Revolution', in Floud and McCloskey (eds) [1981], vol. 1, pp. 164–81.

O'Brien, Patrick and Caglar Keyder, *Economic Growth in Britain and France 1780–1914* (London: Allen and Unwin, 1978).

Ó Gráda, Cormac, 'Supply Responsiveness in Irish Agriculture during the Nineteenth Century', *Economic History Review,* 28 (May 1975), 312–17.

Ó Gráda, Cormac, 'Agricultural Decline 1860–1914', in Floud and McCloskey (eds) [1981], vol. 2, pp. 175–97.

Ohlin, Goran, 'No Safety in Numbers: Some Pitfalls of Historical Statistics', in R. C. Floud (ed.) [1974], pp. 59–78.

Olmstead, Alan, L., 'The Mechanization of Reaping and Mowing in American Agriculture, 1833–1870', *Journal of Economic History,* 35 (June 1975), 327–52.

Olmstead, Alan L., *New York City Mutual Savings Banks, 1819–1861* (Chapel Hll: University of North Carolina Press, 1976).

Olson, Mancur, *The Rise and Decline of Nations: Economic Growth, Stagflation and Social Rigidities* (New Haven: Yale University Press, 1982).

Paquet, Gilles and Jean-Pierre Wallot, 'Crise agricole et tensions socio–techniques dans les Bas Canada au tournant du XIX[3] siècle', *Revue d'Histoire de l'Amérique Française,* 26 (Sept. 1972), 185–237.

Parker, William (ed.), *The Structure of the Slave Cotton Economy of the Antebellum South* (Berkeley: University of California Press, 1970).

Parker, William and Eric Jones (eds), *European Peasants and Their Markets: Essays in Agrarian Economic History* (Princeton: Princeton University Press, 1975).

Parker, William and Franklee Wartenby, 'The Growth of Output before 1840', in Conference on Income [1960], pp. 191–212.

Passell, Peter and Maria Schmundt, 'Pre-Civil War Land Policy and the Growth of Manufacturing', *Explorations in Economic History*, 9 (Fall 1971), 35–48.

Passell, Peter and Gavin Wright, 'The Effects of Pre-Civil War Territorial Expansion on the Price of Slaves', *Journal of Political Economy*, 80 (Nov./Dec. 1972), 1188–202.

Passmore, John, *Hume's Intentions*, 3rd edn (London: Duckworth, 1980).

Patrick, Hugh T. (ed.), *Industrial Growth and Consequences in Japanese Economic Development* (Berkeley: University of California Press, 1976).

Patterson, Donald G., *British Direct Investment in Canada, 1890–1914: Estimates and Determinants* (Toronto: University of Toronto Press, 1976).

Patterson, Donald G. and J. Wilen, 'Depletion and Diplomacy: The North Pacific Seal Hunt, 1886–1910', *Research in Economic History*, 2 (1977), 81–139.

Perkins, Dwight H., *Agricultural Development in China, 1368–1968* (Chicago: Aldin, 1969).

Phelps-Brown, E. H. and Sheila V. Hopkins, 'Seven Centuries of Building Wages', *Economica*, new ser. 22 (Aug. 1955), 195–206.

Phelps-Brown, E. H. and Sheila V. Hopkins, 'Seven Centuries of the Prices of Consumables, Compared with Builders' Wage Rates', *Economica*, new ser. 23 (Nov. 1956), 296–314.

Pincus, Jonathan J., *Pressure Groups and Politics in Antebellum Tariffs* (New York: Columbia University Press, 1977).

Pope, Clayne L., 'The Impact of the Ante-Bellum Tariff on Income Distribution', *Explorations in Economic History*, 9 (Summer 1972), 375–421.

Pope, David H., 'Australian Immigration: A Critique of the Push-Pull Model', *Australian Economic History Review*, 16 (Sept. 1976), 144–52.

Porter, Glenn (ed.), *The Encyclopedia of American Economic History* (New York: Scribner, 1980).

Purdue Faculty Papers in Economic History, 1956–1966 (Homewood, Illinois: Irwin, 1967).

Ransom, Roger, 'Social Returns from Public Transport Investment: A Case Study of the Ohio Canal', *Journal of Political Economy*, 78 (Sept./Oct. 1970), 1041–60.

Ransom, Roger and Richard Sutch, *One Kind of Freedom: The*

Economic Consequences of Emancipation (Cambridge: Cambridge University Press, 1977).

Rapp, Richard T., *Industry and Economic Decline in Seventeenth-Century Venice* (Cambridge: Harvard University Press, 1976).

Ratner, Sidney, 'Taxation', in Porter (ed.) [1980].

Ratner, Sidney, J. H. Soltow and R. E. Sylla, *A History of the American Economy: Growth, Welfare, and Decisionmaking* (New York: Basic Books, 1979).

Rawski, Thomas G., *China's Transition to Industrialism: Producer Goods and Economic Development in the Twentieth Century* (Ann Arbor: University of Michigan Press, 1980).

Reid, Joseph D., Jr, 'On Navigating the Navigation Acts with Peter D. McClelland: Comment', *American Economic Review,* 60 (Dec. 1970), 949–55.

Reid, Joseph D., Jr, 'Sharecropping as an Understandable Market Response: The Postbellum South', *Journal of Economic History,* 33 (Mar. 1973), 106–30.

Reid, Joseph D., Jr, 'Economic Burden: Spark to the American Revolution?' *Journal of Economic History,* 38 (Mar. 1978), 81–100.

Rockoff, Hugh T., 'The Free Banking Era: A Re-examination', *Journal of Money, Credit and Banking,* 6 (May 1974), 141–67.

Rockoff, Hugh T., *Drastic Measures: A History of Wage and Price Controls in the United States* (Cambridge: Cambridge University Press, 1984).

Roehl, Richard, 'Plan and Reality in a Medieval Monastic Economy: The Cistercians', *Studies in Medieval and Renaissance History,* vol. IX (1972).

Roehl, Richard, 'French Industrialization: A Reconsideration', *Explorations in Economic History,* 13 (July 1976), 233–81.

Rosenberg, Nathan, *Technology and American Economic Growth* (New York: Harper and Row, 1972).

Rosenberg, Nathan and L. E. Birdzell, Jr, *How the West Grew Rich: The Economic Transformation of the Industrial World* (New York: Basic Books, 1986).

Rosovsky, Henry, *Capital Formation in Japan, 1868–1940* (New York: Free Press, 1961).

Rostow, Walt Whitman, *British Economy of the Nineteenth Century* (Oxford: Oxford University Press, 1948).

Rostow, Walt Whitman, *The Stages of Economic Growth* (Cambridge: Cambridge University Press, 1960).

Rotella, Elyce J., 'Women's Labor Force Participation and the Decline of the Family Economy in the United States', *Explorations in Economic History*, 17 (Apr. 1980), 95–118.

Rothbard, Murray, *America's Great Depression*, 3rd edn (Kansas City: Sheed and Ward, 1975).

Rothenberg, Winifred, 'The Market and Massachusetts Farmers, 1750–1855', *Journal of Economic History*, 41 (June 1981), 283–314.

Rothenberg, Winifred, 'The Emergence of a Capital Market in Rural Massachusetts, 1730–1838', *Journal of Economic History*, 45 (Dec. 1985), 781–808.

Rudolph, Richard L., 'Economic Revolution in Austria? The Meaning of 1848 in Austrian Economic History', in J. Komlos (ed.) [1983].

Sandberg, Lars G., *Lancashire in Decline: A Study in Entrepreneurship, Technology, and International Trade* (Columbus: Ohio State University Press, 1974).

Sandberg, Lars G., 'The Case of the Impoverished Sophisticate: Human Capital and Swedish Economic Growth before World War I', *Journal of Economic History*, 39 (Mar. 1979), 225–42.

Sanderson, Warren, *The Fertility of American Women, 1800–1975* (New York: Academic Press, 1980).

Saxonhouse, Gary R., 'The Supply of Quality Workers and the Demand for Quality Jobs in Japan's Early Industrialization', *Explorations in Economic History*, 15 (Winter 1978), 40–68.

Scheiber, Harry N., *Ohio Canal Era: A Case Study of Government and the Economy, 1820–1861* (Columbus: Ohio State University Press, 1969).

Schmitz, Mark D., 'Economies of Scale and Farm Size in the Antebellum Sugar Industry', *Journal of Economic History*, 37 (Dec. 1977), 959–80.

Schwartz, Anna J., 'Understanding 1929–1933', in Brunner (ed.), *The Great Depression* [1981], ch. 1.

Shearer, Ronald A. and Carolyn Clark, 'Canada and the Interwar Gold Standard, 1920–35: Monetary Policy Without a Central Bank', in M.D. Bordo and A.J. Schwartz (eds) [1984], pp. 277–302.

Shepherd, James F. and Gary M. Walton, *Shipping, Maritime Trade, and the Economic Development of Colonial North America* (New York: Cambridge University Press, 1972).

Sheppard, David K., *The Growth and Role of U.K. Financial Insti-*

tutions, 1880–1962 (London: Methuen, 1971).

Shlomowitz, Ralph, 'The Search for Institutional Equilibrium in Queensland's Sugar Industry, 1884–1913', *Australian Economic History Review*, 19 (1979), 91–122.

Silver, Morris, 'Karl Polanyi and Markets in the Ancient Near East: The Challenge of the Evidence', *Journal of Economic History*, 43 (Dec. 1983), 795–829.

Smiley, Gene, 'Interest Rate Movements in the United States', *Journal of Economic History*, 35 (Sept. 1975), 591–620.

Smolensky, Eugene, 'The Past and Present Poor', in Fogel and Engerman (eds) [1971] pp. 84–96.

Sokoloff, Kenneth, 'Investment in Fixed and Working Capital during Early Industrialization: Evidence from U.S. Manufacturing Firms', *Journal of Economic History*, 44 (June 1984)a, 545–56.

Sokoloff, Kenneth, 'Was the Transition from the Artisanal Shop to the Nonmechanized Factory Associated with Gains in Efficiency? Evidence from the U.S. Manufacturing Censuses of 1820 and 1850', *Explorations in Economic History*, 21 (Oct. 1984)b, 351–2.

Solow, Barbara Lewis, *The Land Question and the Irish Economy, 1870–1903* (Cambridge: Harvard University Press, 1971).

Solow, Robert M. and Peter Temin, 'The Inputs for Growth', in P. Mathias and M.M. Postan (eds), *Cambridge Economic History of Europe*, vol. vii, pt. 1 (Cambridge: Cambridge University Press, 1978) pp. 1–27; reprinted in Mokyr (ed.) [1985].

Soltow, Lee, *Men and Wealth in the United States, 1850–1870* (New Haven: Yale University Press, 1975).

Spechler, Martin C., 'Regional Concentration of Industry in Tsarist Russia, 1854–1917', *Journal of European Economic History*, 9 (Fall 1980), 401–29.

Steckel, Richard H., 'Antebellum Southern White Fertility: A Demographic and Economic Analysis', *Journal of Economic History*, 40 (June 1980), 331–50.

Sylla, Richard E., 'Federal Policy, Banking Market Structure, and Capital Mobilization in the United States, 1863–1913', *Journal of Economic History* 29 (Dec. 1969), 657–86.

Sylla, Richard E., 'The Forgotten Men of Money: Private Bankers in Early U.S. History', *Journal of Economic History*, 36 (Mar. 1976), 173–88.

Temin, Peter, 'Steam and Waterpower in the Early Nineteenth

Century', *Journal of Economic History,* 26 (June 1966)a, 187–205.

Temin, Peter, 'Labor Scarcity and the Problem of American Industrial Efficiency in the 1850s', *Journal of Economic History,* 26 (Sept. 1966)b, 277–98.

Temin, Peter, *Iron and Steel in Nineteenth-Century America: An Economic Inquiry* (Cambridge: M.I.T. Press, 1964, 1969).

Temin, Peter, *The Jacksonian Economy* (New York: Norton, 1969).

Temin, Peter, *Causal Factors in American Economic Growth in the Nineteenth Century* (London: Macmillan, 1975).

Temin, Peter, 'The Post-Bellum Recovery of the South and the Cost of the Civil War', *Journal of Economic History,* 36 (Dec. 1976)a, 898–907.

Temin, Peter, *Did Monetary Forces Cause the Great Depression?* (New York: Norton, 1976)b.

Temin, Peter, *Taking Your Medicine: Drug Regulation in the United States* (Cambridge: Cambridge University Press, 1980).

Thomas, Brinley, *Migration and Economic Growth: A Study of Great Britain and the Atlantic Economy,* 2nd edn (Cambridge: Cambridge University Press, 1973 [1954]).

Thomas, Brinley, *Migration and Urban Development: A Reappraisal of British and American Long Cycles* (London: Methuen, 1972).

Thomas, Mark, 'An Input-Output Approach to the British Economy, 1890–1914', *Journal of Economic History,* 45 (June 1985), 460–2.

Thomas, Robert Paul, 'The Sugar Colonies of the Old Empire: Profit or Loss for Great Britain?' *Economic History Review,* 21 (Apr. 1968), 30–5.

Tilly, Richard H., 'Mergers, External Growth, and Finance in the Development of Large-Scale Enterprise in Germany, 1880–1913', *Journal of Economic History,* 42 (Sept. 1982), 629–58.

Toniolo, Gianni, 'Effective Protection and Industrial Growth: The Case of Italian Engineering (1898–1913)', *Journal of European Economic History,* 6 (1977), 659–73.

Tortella-Casares, Gabriel, *Los origenes del capitalismo en España* (Madrid: Tecnos, 1975).

Toutain, Jean Claude, *La consommation alimentaire de la France de 1789 à 1964* (Geneva: Droz, 1971).

Tunzelmann, G. N. von, *Steam Power and British Industrialisation to 1860* (Oxford: Oxford University Press, 1978).

Ulen, Thomas, 'The Market for Regulation: The ICC from 1887 to

1920', *American Economic Review*, 70 (May 1980), 306–10.

United States Bureau of the Census, *Historical Statistics of the United States, Colonial Times to 1970,* bicentennial edn (Washington, D.C.: Government Printing Office 1975).

Uselding, Paul J., 'American Manufacturing in the Nineteenth Century', in Porter (ed.) [1980].

Uselding, Paul J. (ed.), *Research in Economic History: A Yearbook* (Westport, Conn.: Johnson, 1976–present).

Uselding, Paul J. and Bruce Juba, 'Biased Technical Progress in American Manufacturing, 1839–1899', *Explorations in Economic History*, 11 (Fall 1973), 51–84.

Vamplew, Wray, 'The Economics of a Sports Industry: Scottish Gate-Money Football, 1890–1914', *Economic History Review*, 35 (Nov. 1982), 549–67.

Vedder, Richard K., *The American Economy in Historical Perspective* (Belmont, Calif.: Wadsworth, 1976).

Vedder, Richard K. and L. E. Gallaway, 'The Geographic Distribution of British and Irish Emigrants to the United States after 1800', *Scottish Journal of Political Economy*, 19 (Feb. 1972), 19–35.

Vries, Jan de, 'Barges and Capitalism: Passenger Transportation in the Dutch Economy', *Afdeling Agrarische Geschiedenis, Bijdragen,* 21 (1978).

Walton, Gary M., 'The New Economic History and the Burdens of the Navigation Acts', *Economic History Review*, 24 (Nov. 1971), 533–42.

Walton, Gary M. and J. Hayden Boyd, 'The Social Savings from Nineteenth-Century Railroad Passenger Services', *Explorations in Economic History*, 9 (Spring 1972), 233–54.

Walton, Gary M. and Ross M. Robertson, *History of the American Economy*, 5th edn (New York: Harcourt, Brace, 1983).

Walton, Gary M. and James Shepherd, *The Economic Rise of Early America* (Cambridge: Cambridge University Press, 1979).

Webb, Steven B., 'Tariffs, Cartels, Technology, and Growth in the German Steel Industry, 1879–1914', *Journal of Economic History*, 40 (June 1980), 309–30.

Webb, Steven B., 'The Supply of Money and Reichsbank Financing of Government and Corporate Debt in Germany, 1919–1923', *Journal of Economic History*, 44 (June 1984), 499–508.

Weir, David, 'Life Under Pressure: France and England, 1670–1870', *Journal of Economic History*, 44 (Mar. 1984), 27–48.

Weiss, Thomas J., 'Urbanization and the Growth of the Service Workforce', *Explorations in Economic History*, 8 (Spring 1971), 241–58.

Weiss, Thomas J., Fred Bateman and James D. Foust, 'Large Scale Manufacturing in the South and West, 1850 and 1860', *Business History Review*, 45 (Spring 1971), 1–17.

West, E. G., 'Educational Slowdown and Public Intervention in 19th-century England: A Study in the Economics of Bureaucracy', *Explorations in Economic History*, 12 (Jan. 1975)a, 61–88.

West, E. G., *Education and the Industrial Revolution* (London: Batsfords, 1975)b.

White, Eugene, *Regulation and Reform of the American Banking System, 1900–1929* (Princeton: Princeton University Press, 1983).

White, Lawrence H., *Free Banking in Britain* (Cambridge: Cambridge University Press, 1984).

Wicker, Elmus, 'Interest Rate and Expenditure Effects of the Banking Panic of 1930', *Explorations in Economic History*, 19 (Oct. 1982), 435–45.

Williamson, Jeffrey G., 'Watersheds and Turning Points: Conjectures on the Long Term Impact of Civil War Financing', *Journal of Economic History*, 34 (Sept. 1974)a, 636–61.

Williamson, Jeffrey G., *Late Nineteenth-Century American Development: A General Equilibrium History* (Cambridge: Cambridge University Press, 1974)b.

Williamson, Jeffrey G., 'Urban Disamenities, Dark Satanic Mills and the British Standard of Living Debate', *Journal of Economic History*, 41 (Mar. 1981), 75–84.

Williamson, Jeffrey and Peter H. Lindert, *American Inequality: A Macroeconomic History* (New York: Academic Press, 1980).

Williamson, Samuel and James F. Shepherd, 'The Coastal Trade of the British North American Colonies, 1768–1772', *Journal of Economic History*, 32 (Dec. 1972), 783–810.

Wright, Gavin, 'The Political Economy of New Deal Spending: An Econometric Analysis, *Review of Economics and Statistics*, 56 (Feb. 1974), 30–8.

Wright, Gavin, *The Political Economy of the Cotton South: Households, Markets, and Wealth in the Nineteenth Century* (New York: Norton, 1978).

Wright, Gavin, 'Cheap Labor and Southern Textiles after 1880', *Journal of Economic History*, 39 (Sept. 1979), 655–80.

Wright, Gavin and Howard Kunreuther, 'Cotton, Corn and Risk in the Nineteenth Century', *Journal of Economic History*, 35 (Sept. 1975), 526–51.

Yamamura, Kozo, *A Study on Samurai Income and Entrepreneurship* (Cambridge: Harvard University Press, 1974).

Yamamura, Kozo, 'General Trading Companies in Japan: Their Origins and Growth', in H. T. Patrick (ed.) [1976].

Yamamura, Kozo (ed.), 'Introduction to Special Issue on Japanese Economic History', *Explorations in Economic History*, 15 (Jan. 1978).

Yamamura, Kozo and Susan B. Hanley, *Economic and Demographic Change in Preindustrial Japan* (Princeton: Princeton University Press, 1978).

Yasuba, Yasukichi, 'The Profitability and Viability of Plantation Slavery in the United States', *Economic Studies Quarterly*, 12 (Sept. 1961), 60–7; reprinted in Fogel and Engerman (eds) [1971].

Yasuba, Yasukichi, 'The Evolution of Dualistic Wage Structure', in H. T. Patrick (ed.) [1976].

Zevin, Robert B., 'The Growth of Cotton Textile Production after 1815', in Fogel and Engermann, (eds) [1971], pp. 122–47.

INDEX